curriculum connections

Psychology

Intellectual Development

BROWN
BEAR
BOOKS

Published by Brown Bear Books Limited

4877 N. Circulo Bujia
Tucson
AZ 85718
USA

First Floor
9-17 St. Albans Place
London N1 ONX
UK

www.brownreference.com

Editorial Director: Lindsey Lowe
Managing Editor: Tim Cooke
Project Director: Laura Durman
Editor: Andrew Solway
Designer: Rob Norridge

Library of Congress Cataloging-in-Publication Data available upon request

Picture Credits

Cover Image
istockphoto

Library of Congress: p. 12 (Metropolitan Printing Co.); Shutterstock: pp. 6 (Stocklite), 9, 14 (Szocz Jozsef), 18 (Frontpage), 21 (Dmitriy Shironosov), 25 (Monkey Business Images), 27 (Svemir), 36 (Dallas Events Inc), 40 (Yulia Ianova), 42 (criben), 45 (Rob Marmion), 46 (Mario Savoia), 51 left (Gregg Williams), 51 right (Jan Martin Will), 58 (alysta), 65 (Specta), 72 (Monkey Business Images), 75 (Alex Kosev), 81 (Tatjana Rittner), 83 (Christopher Hall), 84 (Petrenko Andriy), 86 (Nic Neisch), 91 (Gayane), 93 (Ventura), 96 (Brendan Howard), 99 (Christoprudov Dmitriy Gennadievich), 102 (JustASC); Wikimedia: pp. 10 (Allan Ramsay), 17 (National Institute of Health), 31 (2007 Barsook et al; licensee BioMed Central Ltd.), 33, 37 (Ullmrpvk), 39, 56, 71 (btr), 88 (DuncanCV), 95 (National Portrait Gallery), 105 (Panos Karapanagiotis).

Artwork © The Brown Reference Group Ltd

The Brown Reference Group Ltd has made every effort to trace copyright holders of the pictures used in this book. Anyone having claims to ownership not identified above is invited to contact The Brown Reference Group Ltd.

Printed in the United States of America

Contents

Introduction   4

The Human Computer   6

Attention and Information Processing   18

Learning by Association   32

Representing Information   46

Storing Information   58

Language Processing   78

Problem Solving   90

Glossary   106

Further Research   108

Index   110

Introduction

Psychology forms part of the Curriculum Connections series. Each of the six volumes of the set covers a particular aspect of psychology: History of Psychology; The Brain; Cognitive Development; The Individual and Society; Abnormal Psychology; and Intellectual Development.

About this set

Each volume in *Psychology* features illustrated chapters, providing in-depth information about each subject. The chapters are all listed in the contents pages of each book. Each volume can be studied to provide a comprehensive understanding of the different aspects of psychology. However, each chapter may also be studied independently.

Within each chapter there are two key aids to learning that are to be found in color sidebars located in the margins of each page:

Curriculum Context sidebars indicate to the reader that a subject has a particular relevance to certain key state and national psychology guidelines and curricula. They highlight essential information or suggest useful ways for students to consider a subject or to include it in their studies.

Glossary sidebars define key words within the text.

At the end of the book, a summary **Glossary** lists the key terms defined in the volume. There is also a list of further print and Web-based resources and a full volume index.

Fully captioned illustrations play an important role throughout the set, including photographs and explanatory diagrams.

About this book

Intellectual Development focuses on changes in physiological development from birth through childhood and into old age.

Modern philosophers and psychologists have argued convincingly that the brain shares many characteristics with machines, most notably the computer. This theory is the base of the branch of cognitive psychology known as the information-processing approach.

This volume explores the field of attention and information processing—how the mind may concentrate on a single input, but remains alert to other things. Psychologists are especially interested in the ability to concentrate on more than one thing at a time.

Intellectual Development also examines the ability to learn by association, one of the most important aids to acquiring knowledge. Both classical and operant conditioning are explored.

This volume examines the hypotheses put forward by psychologists to express how the mind might store and represent information. It also analyzes the varying theories about how memory works, considering both short-term and long-term memory and the processes involved in them both.

Intellectual Development also analyzes the fascinating field of language acquisition, including the critical stages in childhood for language exposure and production, and the complex processes involved in speech perception and reading. Finally, the volume explores the ability to solve problems. The subject not only encompasses our approach to questions, but also the processes that lead us to everyday decision making and the way we estimate probability.

The Human Computer

The branch of cognitive psychology called the information-processing approach is based on the idea that the human brain works much like a computer. Obviously there are differences; but efforts to explain the brain in terms of a computer have produced some immensely interesting research.

Mind

The thoughts, perceptions, memories, and emotions that make up human consciousness.

Humans and computers are alike in many ways. Both have a hardware component—the brain in humans and the complex electronic circuitry inside computers. Both also have a software component—the human mind can be likened to computer programs. Both the brain and the mind use this built-in hardware and software to process all sorts of information.

Information processing

Let's examine how we process visual information. Imagine you are at a football game. Sunlight reflects off the surface of objects and flies in all directions. Your eyes collect some of the reflected light and the brain's visual pathways—the hardware—kick into action. Information processing begins. First, the eyes register the incoming stimulation. The cornea and the lens focus and sharpen the image. The light then reaches the retina, where it stimulates light-sensitive cells. The cells transform the light into nerve signals that pass down the optic nerves to the visual cortex at the back of the brain. Information from other parts of the brain—the

Cornea

The clear protective covering on the front of the eye.

Retina

The layer of light-sensitive cells on the inner surface of the eyeball.

Our brains may be physically very different from a PC or laptop, but they operate on similar principles.

software—adds inferences, deductions, and interpretations to what you see. The visual cortex "finishes" the processing by piecing together all the information. At this point—just a fraction of a second after the light from the football field hits your eye—you see the ball being caught in the end zone. Touchdown!

If we accept the proposition that human brains are like computers, information can be defined as any incoming sensory data that passes through the network of neurons that constitute our brains. Light entering our eyes, sound waves entering our ears, and molecules entering our mouth and nostrils are all examples. Information processing is any change to, or transformation of, these data. For this analogy to work, we must also assume that the human brain contains mechanisms, or software, for processing the information. This processing is called cognition and, in its widest definition, encompasses all forms of thinking about the world around us.

The mind as a machine

Cognitive psychologists think that, like computers, our brains act as symbol processors. Computers use binary digits (zeros and ones) to represent information. The numbers are processed by computer programs and switch on tiny pulses of electricity inside the computer. Humans also represent information by symbols, which are processed by the mind. The symbols end up as millions of nerve impulses flying around the brain pathways.

The programs and symbols uncovered by cognitive psychologists are abstract. In our vision example, a physiologist may talk about information being processed in the eye, along the optic nerve, and in the visual cortex. But a cognitive psychologist can describe these three areas equally well—if less specifically—as A, B, and C. In fact, cognitive psychologists often describe everything of importance about visual processing

Visual cortex
The part of the brain dealing with sight.

Curriculum Context
Students may be asked to describe major "schools" of psychology of the 20th and 21st centuries (such as cognitive psychology, behaviorism, Gestalt psychology, and psychoanalysis).

Abstract
Exisiting as an idea but having no physical existence.

without reference to physiology. Building a visual system requires a means to gather the light. Either an eye or a camera will do the job. At the other end software is needed to piece together the processed information. The software must run on a physical computing machine, but cognitive psychologists believe that any general computing device can do it. If this is true, it should be possible to copy the function of the brain using a general computer. All we need to do is feed the computer the same "programs" that the brain uses.

The limitations

Theories of information processing have many critics. One of the charges most commonly leveled is that of reductionism. Psychologists who adhere to the information-processing approach also look to explain complex relationships between an organism, its mind, and its environment in terms of a nonliving object: the computer. This approach may be seen as inaccurate, but the overall benefits are widely regarded as worth the risk.

Any information-processing system is limited in speed and capacity. A program must have a limited capacity to be specific and efficient. For example, no one could read a whole book in one second even if it were possible to see all the pages at once. The brain's "reading program" has neither the speed nor the capacity to do so. Doing too many things at once makes us clumsy and ineffective. The limits of speed and capacity are important components of psychological theories in the information-processing approach.

A science of the mind

The key difference between psychology and other science disciplines lies in the object of study. Traditionally, scientists study physical objects—atoms, electrons, cells, or planets—and the processes that affect them. They draw conclusions and propose theories based on observation. Cognitive studies center

Bottom-up and Top-down

The cognitive system is based on a hierarchy. Information that gets processed, such as auditory and visual stimuli, is at the bottom of the hierarchy. The most complex cognitive systems, such as attention, memory, language, and problem solving, are located at the top of the hierarchy. Thus any level other than the lowest will be a more specific description than the one below it. Any level other than the highest will be less specific than the one above it. Information can flow both from the bottom of the hierarchy to the top, and from the top to the bottom. Moving between levels is a form of information processing.

When information flows from the bottom of the hierarchy to the top, it is known as bottom-up processing. Lower-level systems categorize and describe incoming perceptual information and pass it on to higher levels for more complex information processing. Using the example of vision, the way that light gets processed by the retina, moves along the optic nerve, then activates the cells in the visual cortex is an example of bottom-up processing.

When information flows from the top of the hierarchy to the bottom, it is known as top-down processing. Top-down processing is concept-driven. Perceptual information coming into the system can be influenced by what the individual has stored in the higher levels, for example, information about past experiences.

around a non-physical object: the mind. The information-processing approach allows psychologists to study the effects of the mind more scientifically. Using computer programs, they can test hypotheses about how the mind works and even try to specify the individual processing steps. Indeed, many new discoveries have been made by describing the function of the brain and mind using computer terminology.

One common example of top–down processing is an illusion called the Rubin vase, first developed by Danish psychologist Edgar Rubin. If we have recently been looking at outlines of faces, we will perceive the vase as two black faces staring at one another. If we have instead been recently exposed to pictures of outlines of vases, we will see a white vase. The bottom-up processing of the picture is the same in both cases. But our perception of the image varies according to our memories or past experiences. This is the extreme version of top-down processing.

David Hume argued that the knowledge of cause and effect in a relationship was based on the accumulation of subjective experiences. Thus science, which looks to explain events in terms of cause and effect, is based on the weaknesses of subjectivity.

The modern science of psychology developed from the philosophers of the late 19th century. In 1879 the "father of modern psychology," Wilhelm Wundt (1832–1920), set up the first psychology laboratory in Leipzig, Germany. Wundt relied on introspection as a method of studying mental processes. He set up complex experiments and encouraged people to look at how their conscious experiences changed as a result of the experiment. In this way Wundt believed he could find out how the mind works. Researchers relied on people to report their own observations: the researchers could not observe them directly.

Psychologists soon grew impatient with introspection since the results were flawed in important ways. First, if people report their experiences after the experiment has taken place, they rely on memory, which is not always objective or accurate. Second, people find it difficult to observe their own conscious experiences. They do not have access to the inner workings of mental processes and hence cannot be expected to explain them. Last, introspection produces subjective, not objective, observations.

Innate concepts

The mind does not exist in a physical sense. So how can we study it objectively? The cognitive approach looks at the effect of the mind rather than the mind itself. For example, a fear of spiders is a subjective experience. The enlargement of the pupils and the increase in heart and breathing rate, however, are measurable, physical manifestations of this fear. From there a scientist can work backward to their subjective cause or causes in the mind.

Cognitive psychologists were influenced by a number of prominent thinkers, among them the French

Subjective

A viewpoint that is based on personal experience and opinion. Taste in music, for example, is largely subjective.

Curriculum Context

Students may find it useful to compare Locke's, Hume's, and Kant's views.

mathematician and philosopher René Descartes, the English philosophers John Locke and David Hume, and most importantly the German philosopher Immanuel Kant. Kant suggested that some concepts, such as causality, logic, substance, space, and time, are innate. In modern terms they are programmed into our genes. The mind builds knowledge out of these innate concepts as well as from the accumulation of sensory experiences. These concepts are said to be *a priori* ("from what is before"). The human mind needs *a priori* concepts in the same way as a closet needs hangers to hold clothes.

Innate
Present in all of us from birth.

The transcendental method

Like modern cognitive psychologists, Kant wanted to study these subjective *a priori* concepts objectively. But he recognized that subjective things would remain subjective, just as objective things would remain objective. Anybody who wants to find out the truth about anything must have a preference for objective, unbiased information, because it is naturally closer to the truth. But Kant found a way out of the fix. He proposed a method of reasoning that provided a probable, as opposed to a definitive, conclusion. By sacrificing definiteness, Kant found a way of harnessing subjective data to arrive at an objective conclusion. Kant called this method of reasoning the transcendental method.

Objective
Factual, unbiased information. The lengths and pitches of the notes in a piece of music are objective information. They do not depend on individual taste or opinion.

The transcendental method is also called induction, because the observations come before the explanations. Sherlock Holmes, the fictional detective created by Sir Arthur Conan Doyle, uses this inductive method. In one story, Holmes's friend and companion Dr Watson gives Holmes a pocket watch, and asks him what he can learn from it.

Imagine you are Holmes. Using the transcendental method, you work from observable facts about the pocket watch. For example, it is (a) engraved with the initial *W,* (b) it has a 50-year-old manufacturer's date,

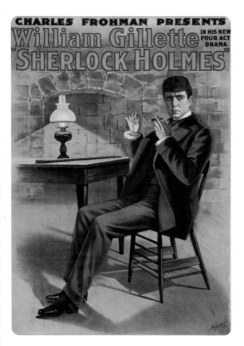

CHARLES FROHMAN PRESENTS
William Gillette
IN HIS NEW
FOUR ACT DRAMA
"SHERLOCK HOLMES"

Sir Arthur Conan Doyle's character Sherlock Holmes applies inductive logic to the crimes he sets out to solve.

and (c) it has several small numbers scratched on the inside of the case. Now you examine each feature and deduce, using existing knowledge of the subject, an appropriate explanation. For example, you combine fact (a), the watch is engraved with a *W* (since the watch comes from Watson, we presume this stands for Watson) and fact (b), the watch is 50 years old. You infer that the watch belonged to Watson's father. However, Watson's father is dead. Inference: the watch was bequeathed to his eldest son (Watson's brother). The scratched numbers (fact c) could have been scratched by a pawnbroker. Inference: the brother had to pawn the watch several times. In each case, we see how the observable facts influence the speculative solution.

Like Kant, cognitive psychologists want to work with objective data. Given a set of facts, the cognitive psychologist can work backward, using the transcendental method, to propose a sequence of information-processing events to explain the facts. These events can then be tested. The methods used are scientific, which means they offer reliability (others can replicate an experiment and obtain the same results) and validity (safeguards prove the test is measuring what was intended and not another phenomenon).

Comparing the mind to a machine using the transcendental method has generated a more complete picture of the mind than any other scientific method.

Reaction times

One of the most commonly used measurements in cognitive studies is reaction time. For example, a researcher could show someone a series of words such as "oxen," "rout," "wont," and so on, and ask the subject to decide if they are real words or not. They may then show a series of words containing "game," "hello," "take," and so on and ask the same question. The first series are all legitimate English words, but they are uncommon. The second series are English, too, but they are more common. The subject's decisions about the common words are likely to be quicker than with the odder ones. This shows in the reaction time. Reaction-time measurement has been a linchpin of cognitive psychology since its beginnings and is likely to remain so for the foreseeable future.

Vision

More than anywhere else, cognitive psychology has made major advances in our understanding of perception. The studies have shown that the human visual processing system is extremely complex and compartmentalized. When artificial intelligence researchers attempted to write programs to instruct machines to "see" like people, problems soon emerged. The machines could be designed to avoid collisions and look for fuel, for example. However, the research indicated that such a machine would need many sensory subsystems to maintain itself in a complex world like our own.

Attention

Our world is a cacophony of feelings, sights, smells, sounds, and tastes. You may be reading this passage, but your mind may be on any number of different things, all of which are conspiring to distract you from the words on the page. Attention provides us with the ability to concentrate on individual bands of incoming information and is therefore an important field of study in cognitive psychology. One example of how attention is important is the "cocktail party effect". At a party you can have a conversation in a crowded room, and the

This boy could be thinking about meeting up with firends, a game of basketball, his birthday party—almost anything. These thoughts are limiting his ability to give attention to his work.

background noise is a meaningless babble. When somebody says your name, however, even though it is part of the background noise, you hear it quite distinctly.

Information-processing research has gone a long way toward explaining some of the mechanisms that underly attention.

Memory

In one sense we are defined by our memories. One way of classifying memory is to divide it into three types. The first is a kind of transitional memory. It refers to relatively unprocessed visual and audio information from the sense organs. The second is short-term (working) memory, which stores a limited amount of data for a few seconds. The third type is long-term memory.

Curriculum Context

Students should be aware of different theories about how memories are stored in the brain.

Many cognitive psychologists think that information is transferred from working memory into long-term memory through the process of examining the information for meaning—the more deeply, the better. Others think that storage occurs as the mind compares new information with data already held in long-term memory. Vital questions remain. Are memories inaccurate or accurate, unchangeable or changeable? And what are the mechanisms by which working memories are processed into long-term memories?

Mental representations

Mental representations have long puzzled philosophers and cognitive researchers. This huge topic underpins many other areas of psychology, including vision, memory, language, and problem solving. Ideas about mental representations are changing. New models suggest that mental representations could be distributed as patterns of activation across neural networks rather than being discrete, separate packages of data. However, some researchers argue that they are the same thing described from two viewpoints. One important notion is intentionality. This theory proposes a distinction between physical objects and mental representations.

Language processing

From an information-processing perspective, language processing is very hard work. Just to convert raw sound waves into speech, then segment that speech, categorize it, and identify its grammar is beyond the most complex computer programs. But a human may hear up to 100,000 words a day and understand nearly all of them. Grammar makes human language distinct from, say, the sign language produced by trained apes. If you read the sentence "Colorless green ideas slept furiously," you know that it is nonsense, but also that it is better formed than "Furiously slept ideas green colorless."

One role of the cognitive psychologist is to try to understand the processes by which people speak and understand speech. Most psychologists think that there are several distinct steps involved in speech. First, the brain organizes what you want to say. Then the grammar is laid out, and finally the individual words are put into a mental map. Understanding speech follows a

Mental representations

The inner representations the mind holds of external objects or ideas.

Curriculum Context

Students should be able to identify the areas of the brain involved in the perception of sound and language.

Curriculum Context

Students may be asked to describe the role of grammar in language systems.

similar pattern of discrete steps. Experiments have also shown that context plays an important role in speaking and understanding speech.

Problem solving

Most human behaviors involve problem solving: finding a sock in a drawer, multiplying two numbers, deciding whether to take the train or the bus. Problem solving and decision making include all mental processes, such as perception, memory, attention, and language. They also form part of what people call thinking.

Gestalt psychologists believe that insight and prior experience were crucial in solving problems. Gestalt psychology rallied resistance to the prevailing behaviorist perspective. Behaviorists argued that problem solving was merely a trial-and-error process in which a successful solution was reinforced and stored in memory. In the 1950s, the mathematician Allen Newell and the economist Herbert A. Simon developed the influential General Problem Solver (GPS), which is based on the assumption that human thought processes are comparable to the functioning of digital computers.

Summing up

The workings of the human mind have been compared to oceans, clocks, puppets, steam engines, telegraph exchanges, and computers as technology has progressed. Will our computer view of the mind be replaced by the next technological advance, the next wonder machine? It is possible but seems unlikely because the comparison between people and machines is a commonplace analogy, and people's brains are frequently compared with computers and their minds with computer programs. Although there are obvious differences, this comparison has proved useful in cognitive psychology and has generated theories in areas such as perception, attention, memory, and problem solving.

Gestalt psychologists

The German word *Gestalt* means "form" or "whole." Gestalt psychologists saw the mind as a whole. They developed their ideas in the late 19th and early 20th centuries.

Behaviorist perspective

Behavioral psychologists argued that the mind could not be studied scientifically: Psychology should only concern itself with the way in which events in the world caused changes in animal (including human) behavior.

Windows on the Brain

Some researchers think that the mind can be understood by examining brain activity under controlled conditions. There is much support for this approach. We know that when the brain is damaged, the mind is damaged. Often if the brain is damaged specifically, the mind is damaged specifically. Also "lower-level" physiological evidence may help cast light on "higher-level" cognitive functions such as memory and problem solving.

Single unit recording

Neurons are the "business cells" of the brain, responsible for all nervous activity. They are the subjects of single unit recording in which a tiny electrode touches a single cell. Neurons pass on information as electrical impulses. At rest a neuron will "fire" several times a minute. When a cell processes information, the firing rate increases. By varying a stimulus—say, a visual one—and varying the neurons studied, researchers can map out which parts of brain become "active" for different visual tasks. This is what the Canadian neurobiologist David Hubel (born 1926) and the Swedish neurophysiologist Torsten Wiesel (born 1924) did together in 1962 to uncover the breathtaking complexity of the visual cortex.

EEG studies

The electroencephalogram (EEG) is a device that measures electrical activity at the surface of the brain. This is a limitation, because it does not necessarily reflect activity deep within. Also, electrical activity in the brain may vary spontaneously. However, it is possible to "blur" the effect of spontaneous activity, leaving only the activity researchers want to focus on. Some researchers compare EEG readings to listening in on a conversation in the next room by putting your ear to the wall. However, it may be used to differentiate between processes that concentrate in separate brain areas. EEGs also show very rapid changes in brain activity.

PET and fMRI scans

When any part of the brain is engaged in a task, this part needs more fuel. This fuel is carried by the blood. For any task, we can begin to see which areas are working harder by monitoring the blood flow. This helps identify the functions of different brain areas. A scanning procedure called positron emission tomography (PET) uses radioactive isotopes to measure blood flow. PET is not very precise, and the timescale of the scans is minutes in duration, so short-lived changes may go unnoticed. A newer technique called functional magnetic resonance imaging (fMRI) can also measure blood flow in the brain. fMRI produces more precise images than PET, and it does not involve using radioactive isotopes. Most modern brain studies use fMRI in preference to PET.

A PET brain scan. PET and fMRI scans like this have given psychologists a 'window' into the mind.

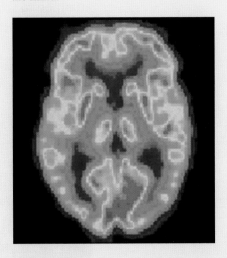

Attention and Information Processing

As you read these words, your senses are receiving information from all around you. Try and think about everything you can see, hear, smell, and feel right now. Can you still concentrate on what you are reading? Your attention has been diverted, and you find it difficult to carry on reading successfully. This shows the importance of attention in performing day-to-day tasks.

Consider a busy intersection during the rush hour. There is too much traffic, and lines quickly build up. The intersection is a bottleneck.

Like the intersection, your brain has a limited capacity to process information. Right now you choose to pay attention to the words on the page. Your brain can easily process this single source of information, enabling you to understand the text. That becomes more difficult if you try to think about the other pieces of information your senses are receiving. You are unable to cope with all this information at the same time.

How do we deal with the brain's limited capacity to consciously process information? You probably consider many of the things around you to be irrelevant, even distracting, as you read this chapter. Therefore you simply ignore them. That is, you use attention to select just the relevant information from what is stacked up behind the attentional bottleneck.

The road over this bridge has limited capacity: it acts as a bottleneck to traffic. The brain's ability to consciously process information forms a similar bottleneck, which limits our ability to pay attention.

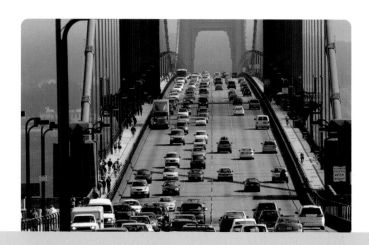

Sometimes it is not possible simply to ignore other information. Imagine you are watching your favorite television program. At the same time, someone is trying to tell you about his or her day. You choose to focus your attention on the TV screen; although you may pretend to be listening and partially take in some of the words, you cannot really concentrate on what the other person is telling you. But what happens to your attention if it is diverted away from the television when the person says something interesting, such as offering you money? You may well have found yourself in a similar position and been accused of selective deafness. This suggests that the mind is capable, in certain circumstances, of attending to more than one source of data, but that it may choose not to do so.

Auditory attention

Many questions about how we focus our attention have been answered by research exploring selective hearing. Our busy lives are filled with hundreds of sights and sounds. It would be impossible for us to interpret and make use of any of them were it not for our selective attention.

To learn more about this, most researchers use the dichotic listening task. Participants wear headphones and listen to two different messages at the same time, one in each ear. They are asked to attend and respond to only one of these messages, ignoring the other.

A typical dichotic litening task was carried out by Colin Cherry, an electronics researcher at the Massachusetts Institute of Technology. People wore headphones and heard a different message in each ear. They had to shadow one of the messages—that is, repeat it back as soon as they heard it. Cherry found that people did not hear the other message (the one that they were *not* asked to shadow). Indeed, participants rarely noticed if the other message was presented backward or in a

Curriculum Context

Students should be able to explain what is meant by attention.

Curriculum Context

Students may be asked to provide examples of selective attention.

Dichotic listening

A procedure used in cognitive psychology that involves listening to two auditory streams, one in each ear.

foreign language. However, they were able to detect physical changes in the subordinate message, such as speech being replaced by a musical tone or changes in the gender of the speaker.

The results of Cherry's experiments address an important question about focusing attention. When does the brain choose which information it will attend to? Does the brain process all the information it receives before selecting what to focus on, or is the information selected first, leaving everything else unprocessed in the data bottleneck?

Filter theory

Dichotic listening studies suggest that the information is selected before it has undergone a great deal of processing. Based on such evidence, in 1958 the British psychologist Donald Broadbent developed a theory of early attentional selection. He called it the filter theory.

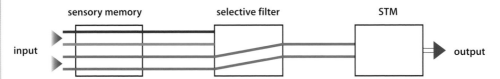

A diagrammatic representation of Broadbent's filter theory of selective attention. STM stands for short-term memory.

Broadbent proposed that a sensory filter selects a message for further processing based on physical characteristics such as pitch or location. The chosen message passes through the filter, leaving everything else behind, where it receives no further processing. Broadbent's filter theory accounts for the findings of Cherry's dichotic listening experiments. In the shadowing task, for example, both messages reach the sensory filter. The target message passes through the filter, while the other message remains unprocessed.

Taking a name check

Imagine now that you are at a party and have focused what you think is your whole attention on the conversation in which you are presently involved.

Suddenly, someone across the room mentions your name. Your attention is immediately redirected. You changed the focus of your attention not because of how you heard the information but because of what that information was about.

According to Broadbent's filter theory, we should not notice details of other conversations because they are filtered out and are not processed by the brain. If this is the case, how could we shift our attention in response to meaning in another message? Could meaning be processed outside our conscious awareness? In 1975 psychologists Elsa von Wright, Paul Anderson, and Evald Stenman presented participants with a list of words, and mild electric shocks were given in conjunction with some of these words. Later, these words were included in "unattended" messages during a dichotic shadowing task. Participants showed a physiological reaction to the words associated with the shocks, even though they were not consciously aware of the words. The implication of the experiment is clear: the participants were obviously interpreting the meanings of the words somewhere in their minds.

People at parties concentrate on the conversations in which they are themselves engaged. Everything else is just background noise—until, that is, someone mentions their name or says something that grabs their attention.

Attenuation theory

Broadbent's filter theory could not explain the results of von Wright and her colleagues. This led Anne Treisman, professor of psychology at Princeton University, to develop a new attenuation theory of selective attention. Treisman retained the idea of a sensory filter at the attention bottleneck. However, she rejected Broadbent's idea that unattended information is simply ignored. Instead, she proposed that unattended messages are attenuated, or weakened, and thus receive a reduced level of processing. However, this processing is so reduced that the participant has no conscious awareness of it unless the meaning takes on some significance.

Treisman's theory accounted not only for the findings of von Wright and others, but also for our ability to redirect attention on the basis of meaning.

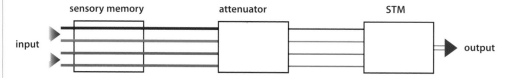

sensory memory　　　　　attenuator　　　　　STM

input　　　　　　　　　　　　　　　　　　　　　　　　　output

Diagrammatic representation of Anne Treisman's theory of attenuated selection, according to which the level of processing applied to input information is increased or reduced by the receiver's view of its importance. (STM stands for short-term memory.)

Broadbent's and Treisman's theories both state that our attentional bottleneck occurs as soon as sensory information enters our brain, before processing occurs. An alternative hypothesis is that all the information we receive is fully processed before selection occurs. Psychologists J. and D. Deutsch suggested in 1963 that it is only after complete processing that we select which piece of information to become aware of.

Subsequent research has suggested, however, that attentional selection is neither early nor late. The way in which attention operates may be flexible, so that the manner of selection depends on circumstances. Late selection may be more likely, for example, when the available inputs are all familiar, relatively slow paced, or involve few decisions about the nature or direction of processing. Early selection may be more likely in the absence of these factors.

Searching for something

So far our discussion of how we focus our attention has explored how we select on what to spend our brain's limited processing resources out of the huge amount of information our senses are constantly receiving. But what if you want to search for something specific: to scan your environment for a particular item, for example a relative you are supposed to be meeting at a busy airport or a friend you are looking for at a very crowded party?

Psychologists have addressed such questions using "visual search" experiments. The main theory used to the findings from these experiments was developed in 1986 by Anne Treisman and is known as feature integration theory (FIT).

Treisman's theory states that, when you look at a visual scene, you create a series of "maps" that describe it. For example, suppose you have a grid of letters containing all Ls and just one T. When you look at the grid, you create one mental map showing where all the horizontal lines are, another showing all the vertical lines, and so on. To find one letter T among many letter Ls, you must mentally search through these maps, combining the horizontal and vertical lines in each position until you find the one that is different. But if there is one letter O among many Ls, instead of the letter T, the search is much easier and faster, because the L and O do not share any features.

In support of her theory Treisman described a phenomenon known as illusory conjunction. If you look out onto a street, FIT states that you create many mental maps, one describing where all the horizontal lines are, another describing where all the red objects are, and so on. You then need to integrate these maps so that, instead of separate features, you see for example a red car. When you look at a busy scene, there are only enough attentional resources available to integrate the features in part of it. Outside this part the integration happens in a fairly random manner, and sometimes features can be incorrectly integrated. For example, a red car passing a white sign on the edge of your vision can be wrongly perceived as a white car. Treisman's FIT theory has inspired research, such as experiments on the perception of texture or features of shapes, that is still being carried out today.

Curriculum Context

Students should be able to identify variables that draw attention to a particular event.

Similarity theory

Treisman's theory has been rivaled by a much simpler theory proposed by John Duncan and Glyn Humphreys in 1992. Their "similarity theory" states that the ease of any visual search is determined by how similar the target is to the other images competing for attention (distracters). So in the two visual search exercises, T is harder to find than O because its shape bears a closer resemblance to that of the distracters. As the target letter and the distracter become more similar, so the difficulty in detecting the target increases. The main criticism of similarity theory is that similarity is a vague concept and there is no agreed measure of what similarity is.

Divided and undivided attention

Sometimes we want to do more than one thing at once. This involves dividing the brain's limited processing resources between tasks. This is easier for some tasks than others. It depends on two main things: how similar the two tasks are, and how good we are at each of them individually. Although the brain has a limited capacity, it can do two tasks simultaneously as long as neither exceeds the limits of its general and specific resources.

Let us first look more closely at our processing resources and how they are allocated. Do all tasks compete for the same limited amount of attention, or do different types of tasks use different mental resources? If all tasks involve the same general resources, the nature of the task would not matter; all tasks would compete equally for a share of the resources available. However, if our processing resources are specific to particular types of task, it will be easier to combine tasks if they are different (for example, driving and talking) than if they are similar (for example, reading a book and talking).

Many studies have shown that divided attention is more difficult if the tasks are similar. In a 1972

Curriculum Context

Students may be asked to describe examples of selective attention and divided attention, and identify variables that influence the ability to divide attention.

experiment, D. A. Allport, B. Antonis, and P. Reynolds asked participants to repeat a passage of text. At the same time, they asked them to memorize either a list of words presented through headphones or a set of pictures. Participants had a poor recollection if they had to memorize words. However, they were able to remember the pictures while repeating the text.

The fact that two similar tasks are difficult to perform together supports the idea that our processing resources are task-specific. That is why we are able to talk while driving. However, consider what happens when at a busy intersection. Can we still continue an important conversation while negotiating the intersection safely? Even if they are dissimilar, we are unable to do two difficult tasks at the same time, which suggests that some of our processing resources are general to all tasks.

Curriculum Context

Students should be aware of how attention differs for demanding versus simple tasks.

The effect of experience

We all know that when we practice something, we become better at it. How does this relate to dividing attention? We have already discussed how easy it is to hold conversations while driving. But that is true only for experienced drivers. Learners generally find it almost impossible to talk while they are at the controls.

Learner drivers have to give their complete attention to the task of driving. They cannot deal with talking or other distractions.

Thus we can see that it is easier to divide attention between two tasks when we are good at them.

To see why, we have to look more closely at exactly what the task of driving involves. You have to pay attention to traffic in front of and behind you, your speed, the course of the road, steering, any potential hazards such as children on the sidewalk, and so on. Can this really be described as a single task?

Virtually any task can be seen as a collection of smaller subtasks. When you learn to drive, all the subtasks of driving seem truly separate. You have to think individually about moving the steering wheel, using your mirrors, your speed, and so on. Thinking about the various subtasks uses up all a novice's attentional resources. The experienced driver is able to handle all the subtasks at the same time without allowing them to interfere with each other.

Every time you learn a new task, you initially have to divide your attention more or less consciously among

The Stroop Effect

Quickly read aloud the following words:

red, **blue**, brown, green, purple.

Now quickly name aloud the colors you see in the sequence below:

green, **blue**, purple, red, brown.

Now, quickly name aloud the colors you see in the sequence below:

blue, **green**, red, brown, purple.

You probably found the first two tasks quite simple. In each the color of the ink corresponded with the word, and so it was easy to read the writing and name the colors. The third task was harder because the colors of the ink differed from the color name. The written words interfered with you naming the ink color. This is known as the Stroop effect.

Originally devised in 1935 by American psychologist John Ridley Stroop (1897–1973), the test has become one of the experiments used most frequently for the study of unconscious, automatic attention. The Stroop effect shows the strong tendency to read the printed word rather than name the color. Because word recognition is so highly practiced, it can proceed automatically. When something is so well practiced that it occurs automatically, we find it difficult to ignore regardless of all conflicting information.

Practice makes perfect. In a 1993 study, Dr. Anders Ericsson of Florida State University found that by age 20 top-level violinists in music academies had practiced a lifetime total of about 10,000 hours.

its subtasks. That demands a large amount of your processing resources. But once you have practiced a task so much that you are expert at it, you no longer need to use up attentional resources—it becomes automatic. Indeed, it is often hard to stop doing things that have become automatic even if you want to. This is central to the "Stroop effect," a task used in research into automaticity (*see* box on page 26).

Cognitive neuroscience

Until recently, psychologists had to rely mainly on experiments to develop their theories about attention. Technological advances now mean we can watch and record attention in action. Attention has been explored in studies using electroencephalographs (EEGs), which record the brain's changing electrical activity. It has also been studied using techniques that allow researchers to watch the blood flow through the brain while participants carry out a task, for instance using positron emission tomography (PET) or fMRI scans (*see* box on page 17).

Brain recording and imaging enable us to explore attention in a different way, allowing us to address different questions. This type of research is known as "cognitive neuroscience." So what lessons can we learn from the study of cognitive neuroscience?

Curriculum Context

Students should be able to describe how the use of scanning and imaging techniques, such as PET scans and fMRI, provides information about the brain.

In 1994 Michael Posner, professor of psychology at the University of Oregon, and Stanislas Dehaene asked the following questions. Do we focus our attention by enhancing our perception of the target above that of everything else around us? Do we suppress our perception of everything but the target? Or does selective attention occur as a result of both enhanced processing of the target *and* suppression of its competitors? From studies using brain scans they concluded that all three possibilities may occur, depending on the nature of the task and the area of the brain involved.

Cognitive neuroscience has also made it possible to look at which attentional processes occur in which areas of the brain. In a 1993 study using PET scans, Maurizio Corbetta and colleagues at Washington University in St. Louis, Missouri, found that the regions of the brain associated with perceiving relevant physical attributes were activated during visual search tasks. For example, when the task involved motion, the brain regions associated with motion perception were activated; when the task involved color, the region associated with color perception was activated.

Attentional disorders

As we have seen, attention is central to our performance of all cognitive tasks. It is no surprise, then, that attention is affected in many disorders of the brain. How do such conditions impact attention and what lessons can we learn from situations in which attentional processes are impaired?

Imagine a fictitious character called Bill with a real condition—neglect syndrome (*see* box). Bill's case study is typical of neglect syndrome patients. A stroke or other damage to one side of the brain leaves patients unable to respond to or have any awareness of anything on the opposite side. The patients also fail to use the left side of their body. This is not because of a

Neglect Syndrome: A Partial View of the World

A man is sitting in a hospital bed. We will call him Bill. Bill has had a stroke in the right parietal (top) lobe of his brain. His doctor walks in and approaches him from the left. Bill doesn't see her or react to her being there. As she moves to the right of him, he greets her as if she had just arrived. The doctor then asks Bill to clap his hands together. He lifts up only his right hand and gestures as if clapping. "What about your left hand?" the doctor asks. Bill replies that he is using it, despite the fact that his left arm remains motionless. Bill's stroke has left him with left-hand neglect syndrome. He is unable to attend to anything in the left half of his visual field. To Bill, anything that happens in his left field of vision no longer exists.

physical motor deficit, just as their inability to attend to visual stimuli to their left is not linked to any sensory deficit. Neglect syndrome is an *attentional* disorder. People with neglect syndrome have "selective inattention" to the left of their world.

Michael Posner and colleagues at the University of Oregon have studied people with neglect syndrome. They found that they can be instructed to attend to their neglected side during attention tasks. From their studies of neglect syndrome, Posner and colleagues suggested a three-stage model of attention. To attend to a stimulus we have to:
• disengage from our current focus of attention;
• shift our attention to the new location; and
• engage our attention with the new task.

People with neglect syndrome have problems with the first stage of attention— they are unable to disengage from the right-hand side of their visual field and focus on their left-hand side.

Attention deficit disorder
Attention deficit disorder (ADD) involves the third stage of the Posner model: People with ADD find it difficult to engage their attention with any one task.

Curriculum Context

Students might be asked to relate examples of research on cortical functioning.

Approximately 4 to 6 percent of children in the United States have a form of ADD. It is caused by immaturity or dysfunction in the attentional control of information processing. In many cases this immaturity improves with time, but around half of those with the disorder continue to experience problems in adulthood.

ADD is characterized by difficulties in concentrating and focusing attention on any task or stimulus. Those affected are easily distracted, impulsive, and hyperactive. Their attentional problems also result in a tendency to find it hard to see a "big picture" linking their world, their thoughts, and their feelings to their actions. This results in fragmented behavior. A child with ADD finds it difficult to concentrate at school, and the behavioral aspects of the disorder can lead to social problems and family difficulties.

PET studies have shown that there is decreased activity in parts of the right hemisphere of the brain in people with ADD. Drugs such as Ritalin have been found to control the disorder. Ritalin works by increasing the amount of certain neurotransmitters, which stimulate the activity of the cortex, including the regions that are underactive. This results in more focused behavior, better concentration, and less distraction.

In the late 1990s the number of children prescribed Ritalin in the United States rose by 150 percent. The United States now uses five times more Ritalin than the rest of the world. The rapid increase in the use of Ritalin has provoked many people to express concern that children are being too quickly labeled as having ADD and being treated with the drug.

Attending to pain
While we have largely looked at attention in relation to how we see and hear the world, it also plays a big role with other senses—particularly in our perception of

Hemisphere

One of the two halves—left and right—of the brain.

Curriculum Context

Students should be able to analyze how the process of neurotransmission can be modified by heredity and environment.

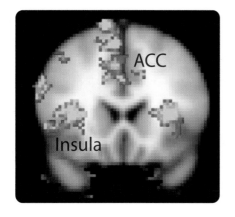 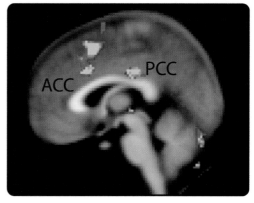

pain. We all experience physical pain from time to time, and PET studies have shown that the anterior cingulate cortex, the area of the brain associated with focusing attention, is highly active when we are in pain. We tend to direct too much attention to the area of our body affected by pain, and knowledge of this tendency can be used beneficially in managing it. Studies have shown that by trying to distract yourself and direct more of your attention elsewhere, you can effectively reduce the awareness of pain. Some people have developed such an ability to control their conscious will like this that they can overcome great pain.

Two functional MRI (fMRI) scans showing areas of the brain that are active during a pain episode. ACC and PCC are the anterior and posterior cingulate cortex.

Conclusions

What can we conclude from our discussion of attention? One thing that is clear is that it plays a critical role in our lives, and that we experience many problems when it is dysfunctional. Cognitive neuroscience and neuropsychology have identified the main regions of the brain associated with attention—the frontal lobes and the anterior cingulate cortex—and research has shown that attention can often be improved with mental training or with drugs like Ritalin. A feature throughout is that attention is central to our conscious existence. It directs and orchestrates our perceptions, thoughts, and feelings, and enables us to carry out the tasks we need to do to live our lives.

Learning by Association

Much of what we learn is the result of conditioning. There are two major types of conditioning: Pavlovian or classical conditioning, and operant conditioning. Conditioning was first observed in experiments on dogs, but it has been observed in other animals and is now known to be present in people.

Learning does not exist in isolation in the brain. Nearly every piece of information in the human mind is associated with something else. When we learn a new concept, fact, or skill, we habitually link it with, and lock it onto, things we know already. Occasionally we may do this deliberately as an aid to memory, but it happens all the time, with or without conscious effort. Psychologists have made a detailed study of the various stimuli that cause this to happen and the responses they evoke.

The structure of knowledge cannot be understood solely in terms of simple associations. Learning—the acquisition and retention of knowledge—is a complex process. Many of the early psychologists who set out to understand it studied animals in laboratories. From these studies, psychologists identified two main types of conditioning—classical and operant.

Classical conditioning

One of the pioneer students of learning was the Russian physiologist Ivan Pavlov. He was originally interested in digestion but broadened his area of study after noticing that dogs would salivate not only when food was set in front of them but also when they anticipated it was going to be. He and his assistants studied what have been termed "mental reflexes" to try and quantify the exact relationship between the presentation of food and the dogs' salivation response.

Curriculum Context

Many curricula ask students to describe the classical conditioning paradigm and to label the elements in classical conditioning examples.

One of Pavlov's many research dogs. Note the saliva catcher implanted in its jaw.

Whenever Pavlov's team used dogs that were new to the tests, all the results were exactly as the scientists expected: the animals salivated when the food was presented to them and not before. But once the dogs gained experience in the laboratory, they began to respond to cues associated with food. One dog would start to salivate as soon as it was brought into the testing room and saw the experimental apparatus. Another dog salivated when a laboratory assistant in a white coat walked past its cage. In neither case had food yet been presented.

Pavlov realized that he had discovered a form of simple associative learning. The dogs had mentally linked the laboratory platform or the appearance of the man in a white coat with the delivery of food. This type of learning is termed classical conditioning.

US and UR, CS and CR

In his experiments with dogs Pavlov called food the unconditioned stimulus (US) and salivation the unconditioned response (UR). The word *unconditioned* is used in both cases to emphasize that the relationship between the two things has not been learned.

Pavlov then conducted learning trials on the dogs. Each trial typically consisted of the presentation of a further stimulus, such as a tone, followed by presentation of the US (food). The trials were brief; for example, the tone would be presented for 10 seconds, and then the food would be brought in. The time between each trial was usually several minutes.

Salivate
Secrete saliva, a watery liquid that aids chewing, swallowing, and digestion.

US
The unconditioned stimulus. For example, food is a stimulus that makes a dog salivate in anticipation of a meal.

UR
The unconditioned response. For example, a dog might salivate in response to the sight or smell of food.

In the first few trials the dog had little reaction to the tone, but salivated in response to the arrival of the food. This was the unconditioned stimulus–response relationship. Later though, the dog salivated when it heard the tone. The tone had thus become a learned, or conditioned, stimulus (CS), and salivation was the conditioned response (CR) to the tone. Pavlov found that, once the CR has appeared in response to the CS, it grows in strength over a number of trials.

Extinction and generalization

The CR will continue only if both the CS and the US keep being applied. The dogs will salivate when they see the man in the white coat only for as long as they associate his appearance with food. But if they see the man repeatedly and no food is presented, the conditioned response will diminish and eventually disappear altogether. This is known as extinction.

When Pavlov used tones to condition the dogs, he noticed that they responded to similar sounds as well as to the exact sound itself. If salivary conditioning was accomplished with a tone of 1,000 Hz, the dog would also salivate when it heard frequencies of 950 Hz and 1,050 Hz, for example. This is generalization of the CR.

General laws of learning

Through his investigation of salivary conditioning in dogs, Pavlov identified and defined the general principles of acquisition, generalization, and extinction. Later investigators confirmed these same phenomena using different procedures. Through being repeated successfully in different experimental situations these principles thus became laws of learning.

Pavlov's research demonstrated that learning can be the result of classical conditioning. Research has shown that there are many other types of learning.

Understanding the procedure

Pavlov's study of salivary responses in dogs established classical conditioning as an important laboratory procedure for the investigation of associative learning. Later investigators developed different classical conditioning procedures, studying other species and response systems. To give just one example, many laboratories have studied the eye-blink response system in adults. Here the unconditioned stimulus–response relationship is that between a puff of air delivered to the eye (the US) and blinking (the UR). The conditioning procedure involves pairing another stimulus, for example, showing a dim yellow light on a screen (the CS), followed by the puff of air to the eye. After several trials the person displays the CR (blinking) when the dim yellow light appears on the screen, before the puff of air.

If an electric shock is the US, the UR will be a feeling of pain followed immediately by a jerk away from the source of the current. This reaction is automatic, predictable, and invariable. Much research has been carried out into whether or not animals can anticipate the shock. Anticipation allows the animals to either avoid the shock or prepare for it, minimizing the effects. This phenomenon is known as fear classical conditioning. In experiments on rats they were first trained to press a lever in order to reach their food, then given electric shocks almost immediately after a light had been flashed in their line of vision. The light thus became a conditioned stimulus—whenever the rats saw it, they recoiled, expecting an electric shock. Later, the same light was shone just as they were about to press the food lever. The result was that they did not press it, implying that the rats do experience fear and anticipate the shock.

Here the unconditioned response is very different from the conditioned response. The UR is an escape reaction, and the CR is the result of fear.

Taste-aversion conditioning occurs when you associate a food with being ill and never eat that food again, even if it was not the cause of your illness. People often make this association between seafood and food poisoning. Taste-aversion conditioning was identified in the 1960s by John Garcia and his colleagues at the University of California, Los Angeles.

Curriculum Context

Students should be able to discuss the adaptive value of one-trial learning, such as Garcia's taste-aversion studies.

Heirarchy

A system in which things or groups of things are ranked one above another according to status.

Desensitization of phobias

Phobias are irrational fears: for example a fear of spiders. In 1924 Mary Cover Jones (1896–1987) of Ohio University reported that by using classical conditioning techniques, she was able to help a phobic child named Peter to overcome his fear. Peter had an irrational fear of rabbits. Jones gave Peter his favorite desserts to eat, and then brought a rabbit gradually closer to him. Over time he began to associate the appearance of the rabbit with the pleasure of enjoying his favorite food. The conditioned stimulus of food and habituation to expect the food with the rabbit canceled out the fear of the rabbit.

In 1958 the clinical psychologist Joseph Wolpe published his work concerning the systematic desensitization of human phobias. He used Jones' work with Peter as the basis for his contention that phobias could be removed. The therapeutic treatment he developed has three steps. First, the therapist and the patient engage in a lengthy conversation about the latter's fears. Together they rank the fears into a hierarchy from the least to the most feared. Next, the therapist teaches the patient a variety of relaxation techniques. They include breathing exercises, muscle stretching, and visualising tranquil places. Finally, while deeply relaxed, the patient is prompted to imagine confronting the fear situations. This starts with the items on the list that cause the least fear and progresses to those that the patient finds the most terrifying.

Wolpe found that more than 90 percent of the phobic people he treated achieved a good or excellent therapeutic result from systematic desensitization.

Instrumental conditioning

In classical conditioning, the unconditional response has to be automatic and involuntary. The psychologist Edward Thorndike identified a learning procedure in which there does not need to be an inborn response , and the animal's behavior is voluntary. This is known as instrumental conditioning.

To demonstrate his theory, Thorndike built a series of puzzle boxes to test a variety of species—most famously cats. The boxes contained devices such as bolts, buttons, latches, levers, and rings. A cat was shut inside the box. If it manipulated the right device, it could escape. Thorndike tested 13 cats, each within its own box. Each box had an escape mechanism different from the others. Thorndike observed the behavior of the cats and recorded the time it took them to escape.

On the first trial each cat would engage in a number of ineffective behaviors, such as hissing, spitting, pacing, and clawing. Eventually—perhaps after several minutes—the cat would manage by a process of trial and error to escape. Trial by trial, each cat made progress. The ineffective responses decreased, and the effective escape response occurred sooner. But progress

Horse trainer Monty Roberts uses classical conditioning techniques on his horses. Here he desensitizes a horse with water phobia.

Operant conditioning

Training a person or an animal to behave in a certain way by punishment or reward.

Curriculum Context

Students should be able to describe the operant conditioning paradigm.

was very slow—the cats learned the way out by trial and error. This was an important finding. Thorndike's results suggested that the cats learned neither through insight nor by applying problem-solving abilities. After the initial blind groping the good efforts were rewarded, and were therefore more likely to be repeated in the future.

Thorndike's explanation of the results was that when a response occurs in a stimulus situation and leads to a "satisfying state of affairs," the response gradually becomes imprinted as a habit. Repeated successes (such as escapes from the puzzle box) lead to stronger and stronger stimulus–response bonds. Ineffective behaviors are gradually dropped, because only effective behaviors are rewarded.

This explanation was formalized by Thorndike as the law of effect. This general law of learning applies to many different species in many different situations.

Operant conditioning

Thorndike's discovery influenced many psychologists, especially B. F. Skinner. Skinner spent many years elaborating Thorndike's learning theories through further experiments conditioning animals in boxes.

Skinner developed a procedure similar to Thorndike's, which he called operant conditioning. In the 1930s at Harvard and the University of Minnesota he constructed a special box to use for experiments studying the behavior of rats. The device is sometimes known as the "Skinner Box," but Skinner himself always referred to it as the operant conditioning chamber. The chamber has a front panel with a metal lever that can be depressed by the rat, and a pellet dispenser that can drop food pellets into a dish. The chamber has several lights that can be turned on and off, and speakers to present auditory stimuli such as tones.

In scientific terms the basis of operant conditioning is a contingency between responding and its consequence. If the rat presses the lever in the operant chamber, it is likely to be given a food pellet: the animal performs the operant, and the probability of reinforcement increases. Prior to conditioning the rats were kept hungry. As a result, they pressed the lever to obtain food pellets many times. Skinner labeled this "reinforcement of the lever-press response."

Skinner studied the behavior of pigeons in an operant conditioning chamber. Pigeons have excellent eyesight, including color vision, and Skinner wanted to study visual discrimination in learning. So his chamber for this purpose contained an illuminated disk that the pigeon was trained to peck in return for food.

Positive reinforcement

Positive reinforcement is achieved simply by providing the subject with something it likes or enjoys. This encourages the animal to repeat a behavior that seems to cause that consequence. There are many examples: a sea lion might get a fish for balancing a ball on the end of its nose, or a child might receive praise and attention for behaving well.

There are two categories of positive reinforcement— primary and secondary. A primary positive reinforcer is something that the animal likes instinctively and does not have to learn about. Such reinforcers include food and the chance to mate. A secondary positive reinforcer is something that the animal has to learn to like. Money, for example, is a secondary reinforcer—it is, as it were, an acquired taste. Adult people may pursue it eagerly, but it would be no good offering money to a three-year-old—she has not yet learned that money can be a desirable commodity.

Schedules of reinforcement

A schedule of reinforcement is the timetable that determines when a reinforcement will be available for the next response, and how often a behavior will result in a reward.

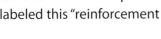

Curriculum Context

Some curricula require students to describe how consequences influence behavior, for example how positive reinforcement strengthens a behavior's occurence.

In a fixed ratio schedule the reward or reinforcement is given only after a certain number of repetitions of the required task. For example, if the fixed ratio is 1:3, every third behavior will be rewarded. Some people are paid on this basis, which is known as piecework: a typist may get $10 for every 100 address labels typed, but nothing for doing only 99 (a ratio of 1:100). This type of schedule may work well, but in some cases removal of the reinforcer will lead quickly to the extinction of the behavior.

In a variable ratio schedule, reinforcers are distributed on the basis of an average number of correct behaviors. A variable ratio of 1:5 means that *on average*, one out of every five behaviors will be rewarded. But when the reinforcer is given can vary, as long as it averages out at one in five over a period. Finally, in a random schedule there is no correlation between the behavior and the consequence.

If people expect to gain a reward at some point, but not necessarily every time they do something, they are not likely to stop after the first few times their action fails to generate the desired result. This is why slot machines remain popular. Although statistically the odds against a payout are high, people keep playing the slots because they think they may get lucky.

If a behavior that has been reinforced in the past stops being reinforced, then that behavior might be extinguished. One way to avoid this is to find a secondary reinforcer. For example, although you might not give your dog a treat every time it sits on command, you should nevertheless reward it with some praise ("Good boy!"). The praise becomes a secondary reinforcer, and after a time can become a substitute for the treat.

There are many other things to be aware of when operating a schedule of reinforcement. If the animal is acting out of fear, you may be rewarding the fear response rather than discouraging the undesired behavior. If, for example, you cuddle a shy dog, it may think you are rewarding it for the very behavior you want to eliminate. Timing is also of the essence. If you teach an animal to stay, then give it a reward after you have said, "Come," it may think that you are rewarding it for the latter behavior rather than the former. Also, the reward must be sufficient to motivate a repetition. Mild praise is not enough for some animals. Also, animals may become sated with the reward you are offering—when they have had enough, it will no longer be motivating.

Positive punishment

Positive punishment aims to reduce behavior by taking away a pleasant treat or something good. If a person or animal enjoys or depends on rewards, it will work to avoid losing them and is less likely to repeat behavior that results in their withdrawal. If, for example, two children have their allowances taken away when they keep fighting, it will give them an incentive to keep the peace. Positive punishment, when applied correctly, is the most effective way to stop unwanted behaviors. Its main flaw is that it does not teach specific alternative behaviors.

Curriculum Context

Students should be able to identify consequences of punishment in controlling behavior.

Sometimes the punishment itself is not needed to reduce unwanted behavior—the threat of punishment may be enough. Such stimuli are known as secondary positive punishers. If, for example, a puppy becomes conditioned to expect a tap on the nose every time it soils the carpet, it may learn to regard a raised hand as enough of a cue to go outside to relieve itself. To be effective, a positive punisher must follow a behavior immediately or be clearly connected to the behavior. Many dog trainers actively condition the word "No!" with some punisher to form an association between the word and the consequence. The conditioned punisher is an important part of training certain behaviors in operant conditioning.

Behaviors are usually motivated by the expectation of a reward. Even with a punishment, the motivation of the reward is often still there. For example, a child may enjoy attention from an adult even though it takes the form of nagging. Or a rat might risk an electric shock if there is the possibility of the reward of food.

Stimulus control

Once a rat has been trained to press a lever for food, its lever-pressing behavior can be brought under stimulus control. Suppose the rat's lever-pressing response is reinforced only when there is a tone being played. The rat will learn to press the lever only while it hears the tone. The tone serves as a discriminative stimulus, and the rat's lever-pressing behavior is controlled by the stimulus of the tone.

Discriminative stimuli such as an on-off tone acquire reinforcing properties. Once the rat has learned that the tone is a discriminative stimulus, it will engage in behavior that produces the tone. For example, suppose the tone is kept off until the rat jumps in the air. When it jumps in the air, the tone comes on, and the rat might press the lever for a food reinforcer, and the tone would turn off again. The sequence or chain of behavior is now: jump–tone on–press lever–food. There are two behaviors and two reinforcers in this chain. Notice that this chain of behavior is built with the terminal behavior first. The rat is first taught to press the lever for food. Then a discriminative stimulus is introduced, and it becomes a conditioned reinforcer. Then another response must occur before the conditioned reinforcer is delivered. Long chains of behavior can be built in this way using conditioned reinforcers and natural reinforcers.

Curriculum Context

Students should understand how operant conditioning can be applied to correct or change behavior, for example by using shaping, chaining, and self-control techniques.

Shaping can be used to train animals such as these dolphins to perform a complicated sequence of behaviors.

Complex behaviors are also taught by shaping. This involves initially reinforcing behavior that roughly corresponds to what is desired. Gradually, the animal has to perform the desired behavior more and more accurately in order to gain a reward. This technique has been used to train performing animals.

Behavior therapy

B. F. Skinner was greatly interested in behavior therapy and behavior modification—the application of operant conditioning to the modification of problem behaviors. In 1948, while at Indiana University, he inspired fellow graduate student Linda Fuller to apply operant principles to an institutionalized 18-year-old who had been diagnosed as feebleminded. The man spent his time lying in bed, not moving or making a sound. He refused to eat or drink, so had to be force-fed. Fuller treated him with a milk reinforcer, which was directly injected into his mouth. Using continuous reinforcement, she succeeded in training him to make movements with various parts of his body.

In 1963 a psychologist named Teodoro Ayllon, also under Skinner's tutelage, worked with an institutionalized psychotic woman who had a nine-year history of stealing and hoarding towels. Following Ayllon's instructions, the staff gave her many towels whenever she stole one. She eventually had 650 towels in her small room. At this point she started removing the towels from her room. The reinforcing value of the towels had been reduced by giving her so many.

In 1968 Ayllon and Nathan Azrin established what they called a token economy at Illinois State Hospital, a facility for female schizophrenics. The women earned plastic tokens for engaging in desirable behaviors, such as making their beds and eating properly. The tokens were then exchanged for privileges, such as being able to take a long walk in the grounds, and for desired

Curriculum Context

Some curricula expect students to be able to discuss Skinner's contributions to popularizing behaviorism.

items, such as candy. Using Skinner's definition, the tokens were conditioned reinforcers. Ayllon and Azrin found that desirable behaviors increased dramatically. When the tokens were removed, the desirable behaviors decreased. Finally, when the tokens were reintroduced, the desirable behavior increased dramatically once again.

Another technique is to measure physical functions such as heart rate or blood pressure, amplify them, and show them to the person as a sound or in some other form of representation. This has been successful in helping people control a particular reaction, for example, in stressful or frightening situations.

Current applications

Skinner's contingencies of reinforcement have had dramatic success in modifying various undesirable behaviors, such as overeating, smoking, shyness, speech problems, and autism. Many residential programs for people with learning difficulties employ operant conditioning principles as part of the treatment. Although some people applying Skinner's work have used punishment and aversive procedures, Skinner was against such practices and always advocated reinforcement. He argued that, although punishment teaches individuals that a certain behavior is inappropriate, it does not show them the correct way to behave.

Objections

Some people object to behavior therapy on ethical grounds. First are the objections to the use of unpleasant stimuli, for example in aversion therapy. Second are concerns about depriving people of the right to choose how they behave. Another objection is that the effects of this mode of therapy or learning are short-lived. That is because it treats the immediate behavior rather than the underlying problem.

Curriculum Context

It might be useful to identify and discuss ethical issues in psychological research.

Reinforcement can have applications in education. For example, children might earn tokens for obeying certain well-defined rules. The tokens are secondary reinforcers since they are exchanged for a desired activity such as reading a favorite book or getting time on the computer. Teacher approval can be a powerful positive reinforcer.

The central proposal of both Pavlovian and operant conditioning is that there are general principles of learning covering a wide range of species in various situations. Most of the theories of learning are derived from experiments conducted on animals in a laboratory. Skinner, for example, wrote a book solely about key-pecking in pigeons but was convinced that the findings could be generalized, so he entitled it *The Behavior of Organisms*. Critics say that these results cannot be transferred automatically to people, who have more complex nervous systems, and who are capable of thought. Certain forms of learning are specific to a particular species, or depend on what is being learned. An example is language learning in humans (see chapter 6, page 78). Some learning principles cannot be universally applied.

In spite of the criticisms and the fact that few psychologists totally accept conditioning techniques today, the legacy of the behaviorists has been to contribute significantly to the development of learning theory and therapy.

Representing Information

Our brains can hold an enormous amount of information. Most people know how to read, write, and say thousands of words; we know how to get from our homes to dozens of different places; psychologists have shown that we can remember thousands of different pictures. A great deal of research into the brain focuses on how it stores and represents this wealth of data.

In the modern world all sorts of devices represent information. Some, like books and maps, have been around for thousands of years. At the other extreme, the World Wide Web did not exist until 1993, although the Internet has been around for several years longer. However, even the oldest book is a newcomer compared to the brain. The human brain has been representing information for millions of years.

From above, a city looks like a meaningless jumble of buildings. On a map, the underlying street plan is much clearer, because the mapmakers omit unnesessary information.

Psychologists describe maps, books, and pictures as external representations. They are distinguished from internal representations, which are the ways that the brain stores and retrieves potentially useful information.

Pictures in the brain

People have theorized about internal representations for centuries. The ancient Greek philosopher Aristotle argued that memory was like storing pictures in the head. In 1883 the English scientist Francis Galton investigated the imagery used by the brain by asking a number of eminent friends to imagine the way their breakfast table had looked that morning. Quite a few said they had no mental picture of their breakfast table. They could remember what they had eaten, but did not think they had a picture of the table in their heads.

Psychologists now know that people *can* generate mental images. Techniques that map brain function, such as functional magnetic resonance imaging (fMRI), show which parts of a person's brain are most active. When people look at pictures, a part of the brain called the primary visual cortex becomes very active. Researchers have found that when you ask people to imagine a picture they have just seen, the primary visual cortex becomes active again. The same regions of the brain are highly active both when we see a picture and when we are are imagining it.

People are good at forming mental images. We can also imagine new images, and manipulate them in our heads. In 1975 the American psychologist Stephen Kosslyn asked people to imagine a particular animal with another one standing next to it. For example, he asked someone to imagine a rabbit sitting next to an elephant. He then asked a question about the rabbit, such as "Does the rabbit have a pointed nose?" Kosslyn then asked a different person to imagine a rabbit, but this time with a fly sitting next to it. He asked that person the same question.

Kosslyn found that people took longer to answer questions about the rabbit if it was standing next to the elephant. When the subjects in the experiment made mental images, they had to "zoom in" or "zoom out" to fit both animals in. The mental image of the rabbit is larger when the animal next to it is a fly rather than an elephant. Kosslyn showed that the time taken to answer questions about mental images was closely related to the amount of "zoom" required to bring details into view.

Mental images do not represent what we have seen; rather, they represent our interpretation of what we have seen. In 1985 psychologists Deborah Chambers and Daniel Reisberg demonstrated this in an elegant

Curriculum Context

Students may be asked to discuss how the use of new technologies provides information about the brain.

Curriculum Context

Students may be expected to identify mental images as an element of the process by which people manipulate and understand information.

Is this a duck, or is it a rabbit? The duck–rabbit experiment works best if the subject has never seen the object before. Try showing it to friends to see how they interpret it.

yet simple experiment. Show the image on the left to a friend very quickly, then ask them what the picture showed, and whether there was anything else it could be. Next, ask your friend to draw the image as they remember it on a piece of paper. Then ask the questions again. Most people think that the original picture shows either a duck or a rabbit. No one in the experiments could "see" both the duck and the rabbit in their mental image. However, almost all people could see the other animal once they had drawn it.

Mental images tend to have a fixed interpretation, while pictures and photographs in the outside world do not. The images that appear in our minds cannot be described simply as internal photographs. These pictures are internal representations, and meaning is an important part of that representation.

Mental maps

As we have seen, mental images are as much about interpretation as photographic accuracy. So, if our brains represent photographs like maps, do they represent the information provided by external maps in a similar way? People are normally pretty good at remembering how to get from A to B. For example, you may know that to get from the swimming pool to your house, you go over a bridge, up the hill, follow the street around, and turn right at the corner. However, although you know the way to the swimming pool from home, would you be able to point in the direction of the swimming pool? The

Mental pictures are short-lived, as an experiment by Morton Gemsbacher demonstrated. She showed one of a pair of images like these to a group of subjects. Ten minutes later she showed them both images and asked which one they had already seen. People's answers were statistically no better than guesswork.

answer is "probably not" unless you had a map. In 1982 Perry Thorndyke and Barbara Hayes-Roth demonstrated the inaccuracy of most people's mental maps. They interviewed secretaries working in a particularly large and complex office building. They found that even those who had recently arrived could accurately describe how to get from A to B. For example, they had no difficulty giving directions from the coffee room to the computer center. However, new secretaries were often unable to indicate the straight-line direction of the coffee room from the computer center. Generally speaking, only secretaries who had worked in the building for several years could do this.

Curriculum Context

It might be interesting to think of examples of your own mental maps, such as of your home, classroom, school, or neighborhood.

Dictionaries in the brain

Dictionaries store information about objects (nouns), (verbs), and abstract concepts like democracy. People also store much of this information in the brain. Does the brain represent this information in the same way that dictionaries do?

Writers of dictionary entries aim to present a list of defining attributes or features. For example, the *Cambridge English Dictionary* defines an elephant as "a very large gray mammal which has a long nose (trunk) with which it can pick things up." Gottlob Frege (1848–1925) was the first to suggest that all concepts could be described with a set of defining attributes. The "defining attributes" theory is best explained by example. Think of the word bachelor. The defining attributes of this concept are "male," "single," and "adult." Each attribute is "necessary." If any is missing, the person cannot be a bachelor. Together the three attributes are "sufficient." If someone is an adult, single male, he is a bachelor. The idea that all visible objects and concepts could be represented by defining attributes came to dominate philosophical and psychological thinking for a time but was strongly opposed by Ludwig Wittgenstein (*see* box on page 50).

Ludwig Wittgenstein

Ludwig Wittgenstein (1889–1951) was one of the most influential philosophers of the 20th century. He was born in Vienna, Austria, and originally trained as an engineer. In 1908 he moved to Manchester, England, where he was paid to experiment with kites. Later, he became fascinated by philosophy, and studied with the famous British philosopher Bertrand Russell (1872–1970). In 1922 Wittgenstein published *Tractatus Logico-Philosophicus*, a work that was to have a profound influence on many philosophers and psychologists.

The summit of Wittgenstein's achievements was his book *Philosophical Investigations*, which was published after his death. It made a major contribution to our understanding of mental representation. Before its publication psychologists thought that all concepts could be represented by a set of defining attributes. A bachelor was "adult," "single," and "male." In the same way there were defining attributes for birds, chairs, and democracy. In *Philosophical Investigations* Wittgenstein challenged this idea. He contended that many concepts do not have defining attributes.

Wittgenstein's way of thinking about concepts opened up a whole new area of psychological research. The work of a number of later researchers, such as Eleanor Rosch, can be seen as developments of his ideas.

Curriculum Context

Students should recognize that information is classified into categories containing similar properties known as concepts.

Psychologists describe groups of objects that share certain defining characteristics as "categories." The objects that make up categories are called "members." The views of Frege led to the conclusion that all objects must be classified as either members or nonmembers of a particular category. Membership in a category is all-or-nothing; there are no shades of gray.

However, the decisions people make when allocating objects to categories do not seem to follow this rule. Psychologists Michael McClosky and Sam Glucksberg asked people whether certain objects belonged to the category "furniture." Everyone agreed that chairs were furniture and that cucumbers were not. When they came to bookends, however, some people thought that they were furniture, while others did not. In addition, people were inconsistent about their definitions. The researchers asked people about objects like bookends on a number of occasions. Some people said that bookends were furniture the first time they were asked but not the second, or vice versa.

If people's mental dictionaries contained lists of defining attributes, subjects should have been in complete agreement about whether bookends were furniture, and decisions about common categories would be consistent.

The research of Eleanor Rosch revealed further problems with the defining attribute view. If the mental dictionary is simply a list of defining attributes, there should be no such thing as a good or a bad example of something, such as a bird. All objects should either be birds or not birds. Rosch asked people to rate how typical they thought various members of categories were. People generally agreed on typical and atypical members. For example, they agreed that robins were typical birds but that penguins were not. If people's mental dictionaries were as Frege suggested, there should be no such thing as a typical bird.

A robin and a penguin—which is the more "typical" bird? The work of Eleanor Rosch suggests that most people think of a robin as an example of a typical bird, but do not think the same of a penguin.

This and further experiments Rosch carried out suggested that when people are asked to think about a category, they do not think of a list of defining attributes. Instead, they think of typical members of that category.

Hierarchies

We have seen that a dictionary defines an elephant as "a very large gray mammal." In dictionary definitions words like mammal are quite common. Dictionary writers try to define objects as part of a "hierarchy." If you look at the diagram below, you will see that at the top of the hierarchy is the term "animals." Both birds and mammals are types of animals, so they sit below "animals" on the hierarchy and are connected to it by downward arrows. Robins and penguins are both types of birds, so they are connected to "bird." In the same way "elephant" and "dolphin"are both connected to "mammals." Dictionary writers use hierarchies because they help shorten definitions. If the dictionary states that "a robin is a bird," the reader knows that a robin has feathers and wings, and that the female lays eggs. The dictionary does not need to include this information. Might the brain use the same trick to reduce the amount of information it has to store?

Allan Collins and Ross Quillian argued that the answer was "yes." They presented a series of sentences like this to students:
• Canaries can sing.
• Canaries have feathers.

The students were quick to agree that canaries could sing. They took longer to agree that canaries had feathers. If the brain were organized like a dictionary, that is exactly what you would expect. If you look up "canary," the dictionary will tell you that "canaries can sing." Not all birds can sing, so singing has to be part of the definition. However, feathers are part of the definition of a bird, which is one step up the hierarchy. You have to "look" in two different places, which takes

Curriculum Context

Students should be able to examine the role of hierarchies in organizing concepts.

An example of a hierarchy.

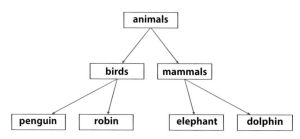

measurably longer. Another group of psychologists—
Edward Smith, Edward Shoben, and Lance Rips—gave
students a slightly different series of sentences. Two of
the sentences that the researchers used were:
• A chicken is a bird.
• A chicken is an animal.

If the brain was like a dictionary, it should take longer
to check the second sentence than the first. To check
that a chicken is a bird, you just need to look up the
definition of "chicken." To check that a chicken is an
animal, you also need to look up the definition of "bird."
The researchers showed that the opposite was true.
People took longer to agree that a chicken was a bird
than they took to agree that a chicken was an animal.

This result fitted with Eleanor Rosch's research showing
that some category members are more typical than
others. According to her research, a robin is a typical
bird, but a chicken is not. So agreeing that a chicken is
a bird takes longer than agreeing with the sentence
"A chicken is an animal."

Mental dictionaries

We are not sure how the brain
stores information. One popular
idea is that the brain's dictionary is
pretty disorganized. Our mental
dictionaries do not contain a long,
neat list of definitions. Instead, our
knowledge is held within a mass
of connections between small
chunks of information. Psychologists
call these chunks features. Some of the
features of being a dog might be "furry,"
"four-legged," and "having a wagging tail." We learn
things like this about dogs when we are young. Our
brains store this information by forming links between
features like "wagging tail" and labels like "dog." The

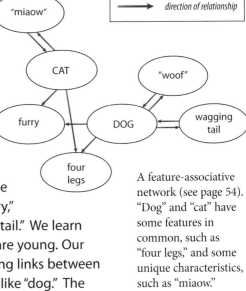

A feature-associative
network (see page 54).
"Dog" and "cat" have
some features in
common, such as
"four legs," and some
unique characteristics,
such as "miaow."

diagram on page 53 shows part of our mental dictionary. This sort of association is described by psychologists as a feature-associative network.

Another popular idea about our mental dictionary is that it is filled with examples. According to this theory, your dictionary entry for "dog" is just a collection of particular dogs you have met. It might include a description of your pet dog, Lassie, your neighbor's dog, and the guard dog you once saw at a factory. Your dictionary entry for "cat" is similar.

Scripts and themes

A dictionary will tell you what eggs and flour are, but it will not tell you how to bake a cake. To find that out, you need to look in a cookbook. Cookbooks are just

Learning from Doodles

We have already looked at how the information in the mental dictionary is organized, but how does this information get there in the first place? One way to study this is to teach adults new categories. To make sure the categories are new for everyone, psychologists often use made-up ones. A 1981 experiment by Donald Homa, Sharon Sterling, and Lawrence Trepel provides a good example of this. The researchers invented three different doodle categories. They set aside some of the doodles, and showed the rest to college students. They taught the students to recognize which of the

three categories each doodle came from. When the students had mastered this, the psychologists took the doodles they had put to one side and asked the students to decide which category each of these "new" doodles belonged to. The college students were fairly good at doing this, but not as good as they were with the original doodles. The students found the old doodles easier to deal with because they had information about them in their mental dictionaries. They had not seen the new doodles before, and so they had not been entered into their dictionaries.

  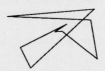

Some examples of the doodles used by Homa and his colleagues in their 1981 study.

one example of the wide range of instruction manuals that people rely on. They tell us, step by step, what we have to do to complete a task.

Does the brain store information about everyday processes in an "instruction manual"? Roger Schank and Robert Abelson suggested that people use mental scripts for occasions such as going to a restaurant. Scripts are a list of the typical events that occur in a specific situation. For example, the script for a trip to a restaurant might be:

Enter restaurant. Go to table. Sit down. Get menu. Look at menu. Choose food. Give order. Wait and talk. Waiter delivers food. Eat and talk. Receive check. Pay check. Leave.

Obviously, not all restaurant trips are exactly like this. A script does not tell you for sure what will happen, but it does tell you what is likely to happen most of the time. Scripts also help us communicate with other people more efficiently. If you ask someone what they did last night, and they reply, "I went to a restaurant," your restaurant script will provide you with an idea of the series of events the person experienced.

People's memories of specific events are affected by their mental scripts. Psychologists Gordon Bower, John Black, and Terrance Turner carried out an experiment in which they gave people some stories to read. The stories were based on scripts such as "going to a restaurant," but the psychologists had jumbled the order of some of the events. When people were asked to remember the stories, they often described what normally happens in a restaurant, rather than what actually happened in the story. So although mental scripts help us anticipate what will happen in certain situations, they may also color our recall of what happened in reality.

Curriculum Context

Students should be able to describe the processes that lead to inaccuracies in memory.

In another experiment Bower gave people several different stories to read. Later, he gave the same people a different set of stories. Some stories were exactly the same as before, others were not. The researchers asked the volunteer readers to decide which stories were new. The volunteers were generally good at this, but if a story was new but described an event similar to an old story, the subjects sometimes thought they had read it before. They became confused by stories that had similar but related scripts. For example, one of the original stories involved a trip to the dentist. Later, the subjects read a story about a visit to the doctor. The volunteers would often believe that they had read the story before.

This research suggests that people remember stories in terms of general themes that are less tied to a specific situation than to a script. For example, most people would say that the 20th-century musical *West Side Story* is similar to William Shakespeare's 1595 play *Romeo and Juliet*, despite the fact that they are set in different countries and in different centuries. (In fact, *West Side Story* was based on *Romeo and Juliet*.) Roger Schank has argued that the stories share the common theme of "mutual goal-pursuit against outside opposition."

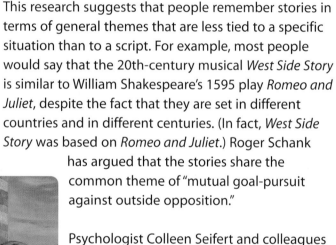

The balcony scene from *Romeo and Juliet*, as imagined by Ford Madox Brown. The film *West Side Story* is based on the story of Shakespeare's play.

Psychologist Colleen Seifert and colleagues showed people a series of stories that differed in many details but that all had the same general theme. Once the subjects had read the stories, the researchers asked them to write out similar stories. Most wrote stories that contained different details but had the same general theme. Seifert's team also gave people a set of stories to sort into different piles. The subjects were allowed to do this in any way they wanted, but most sorted them into common themes.

Frederick Bartlett

Sir Frederick Bartlett (1886–1969) was one of the founders of modern psychology. He joined the Laboratory of Experimental Psychology at Cambridge University, England, as an assistant in 1914. By 1931 he was a professor and head of the laboratory. By the close of World War II Bartlett's former students were running the majority of psychology departments in the UK.

Bartlett fought hard to get psychology recognized as a scientific subject. His success had a profound influence on 20th-century psychology. He is probably best remembered for his ideas about schemata. A schema is a piece of general information stored in the brain that helps us understand the world around us. For example, the restaurant script (*see* page 55) is a schema. Bartlett's ideas about schemata were largely ignored in the United States at the time but have subsequently been included in many textbooks.

Information and the brain

For most of the 20th century psychologists have relied on metaphors to explain how the brain stores information. The mind has been equated with a photograph album, a dictionary, and a playscript. Many psychologists now believe that theories about the mind should take into account how it really works. The brain does not contain dictionaries, maps, or pictures. It contains nerve cells (neurons), which communicate through electrical signals—nerve impulses.

We know quite a lot about how neurons interact and a little about how they store information. For example, we know that, compared to modern computers, neurons work very, very slowly. We also know that neurons work in a "massively parallel" way. When you look at a picture, some neurons detect horizontal lines, some detect vertical lines, and others look for diagonal lines. They all do this at the same time, as well as carrying out a multitude of other functions. Connectionist theories incorporate biological features of the brain. The theories often include mathematical principles to describe how neurons communicate with and learn from each other.

Metaphor

A figure of speech in which a word or phrase is used to mean something other than what it literally means.

Curriculum Context

Students should be able to describe how information is transmitted and integrated in the nervous system.

Storing Information

In recent times a great deal of research has been conducted on human memory. Without memory we would not be able to do many of the simple, everyday tasks that we take for granted. We now know that memory is not just a passive receiver of information but an active process that makes deductions about information and reconstructs events.

Curriculum Context

Students should examine the influence of the theories of Plato and other Greek philosophers on later Western studies of the mind.

The ancient Greek philosopher Plato thought that memory was like a wax tablet on which impressions were made (encoded) and then stored so that we could return to, or retrieve, them at a later time. Other ancient philosophers likened memories to birds in an aviary or to books in a library. Contemporary theorists such as Ulric Neisser, Steve Ceci, Elizabeth Loftus, and Ira Hyman have come to appreciate that memory is a selective and interpretive process. These psychologists have all carried out experiments to show that memory reconstructs, integrating prior beliefs and expectations with information (including misleading information) that was given at the time of encoding.

It is not possible to remember everything that we experience. We need to remember some things in order to function effectively in the world, but there are other things that we do not need to remember. Our memory works like a filtering

Ancient philosophers drew comparisons between memories and birds in an aviary. The problem was to retrieve the right memory once it had been stored, just as it is difficult to catch a particular bird.

mechanism, ensuring that we do not remember absolutely everything. We can also select, interpret, and integrate our memories. Most contemporary researchers view memory as an active rather than a passive thing.

The logic of memory

Any effective memory system—whether it is a video recorder, the hard disk of your computer, or even a simple filing cabinet—needs to do three things:
- *encode* (take in) information;
- *store* or retain that information faithfully and, in the case of long-term memory, over a significant period of time;
- *retrieve* (be able to access) stored information.

All three components have to work well together if our memory is to perform efficiently.

Memory can fail to work due to a blockage in any or all of these three components. If we do not pay attention when we are presented with information, we may not

A Perfect Memory

In his book *The Mind of a Mnemonist* (1968), the psychologist A. R. Luria details the following case. In the 1920s Shereshevskii (S) was working as a journalist. His editor noticed that he was very good at remembering instructions. However complex the briefing he received, he could repeat it back almost word for word. The editor persuaded S to see Luria for tests. Luria set a series of increasingly complex memory tasks, including lists of more than 100 digits and long strings of nonsense syllables. S could repeat this material perfectly even in reverse order. He could also recall the information several years later. His secret seemed to be twofold. He was able to create a wealth of visual images without much effort. He also had the power of synesthesia, which means that words or sounds evoke specific smells or colors. Information that appeared dry and dull to other people created a vivid sensory experience for S.

Unfortunately, his abilities had a negative side. S became more and more distracted by his memories. He left journalism and became a professional mnemonist, demonstratng his extraordinary skills on stage. He became increasingly unhappy, however, as his memory filled up with useless information.

A Computer Analogy

Working memory is sometimes likened to the random-access memory (RAM) capacity of a computer. When you turn the computer off, any information in the RAM is lost. The hard drive of the computer is like long-term memory. Information put there remains stored when the computer is switched off and can be kept indefinitely. Switching off power is like falling asleep. When you wake up after a good night's sleep, you still have access to information stored in your long-term memory, such as who you are or what happened on an especially eventful day in your personal past. But typically, you cannot remember the last thoughts you held in your working memory before you went to sleep.

Curriculum Context

Students should be able to analyze the importance of retrieval cues in memory by examining problems related to retrieval such as the tip-of-the-tongue phenomenon and context effects.

encode it efficiently or we may not encode it at all. If we do not store the information effectively, we say that we have forgotten it. With retrieval an important distinction is often made between availability and accessibility. For example, sometimes we cannot quite recall someone's name; it is "on the tip of our tongue." In this "tip of the tongue phenomenon," or TOTP, the information is stored somewhere. It is, in theory, potentially available, but it is not currently accessible—we fail to recall it.

The processes of memory

One of the major findings of the last hundred years is that there are different types of memory. The main three types are the sensory store; short-term (working or primary) memory; and long-term (secondary) memory.

Consciousness

The mind's awareness of itself and the world.

The sensory store appears to operate below the threshold of consciousness. It receives information from the senses and holds it for about a second. With sensory memory what we ignore is quickly lost and cannot be retrieved. However, you can sometimes catch an echo of something sensed when you were not paying attention. For example if you are deep in conversation at a party, then someone mentions your name elsewhere in the room, your attention is automatically diverted.

Paying attention to something transfers it to working memory, which has a limited capacity of around seven items plus or minus two. This store is used when, for example, you dial a new phone number. Old information is displaced by any input of new information. Less important items—such as a phone number you have to call only once—are held in the working memory, used, and then discarded.

Continuing to process information transfers it to long-term memory, which seems to have almost unlimited capacity. Long-term memory is the primary focus of this chapter.

The modal model of how the sensory memory, short-term (working) memory, and long-term memory are linked.

Previously people believed that working memory was a passive process, but we now know that it does more than just hold information. Psychologists now generally accept that people can do information processing or manipulation in working memory while at the same time holding information in four or five memory slots.

Levels of processing

In 1972 experimental psychologists Fergus Craik and Robert Lockhart developed the "levels of processing" framework, which was to have a great influence on later theories about memory. Its key principle echoed Marcel Proust: "We soon forget what we have not thought about." Craik and Lockhart's experiments tested people's ability to remember things after a time lapse. They showed that "deeper" processing of information is superior to more "superficial" processing. They also showed that elaboration of material can improve our ability to memorize items.

What does this mean? Suppose you were asked to study a list of words and then tested on your memory

Curriculum Context

Students may be required to characterize the difference between surface and deep (elaborate) processing.

of them. Typically you would remember more of them if you defined each word on the list, or gave each one a personal association—this technique is known as elaboration of material. You would remember fewer of them if you provided a rhyme for each word or gave each letter a number reflecting its position in the alphabet, because these are more superficial tasks in semantic terms.

According to the levels of processing theory, if a particular operation or procedure produces better memory performance, it arises from a deep mode of processing. Conversely, if another operation or procedure shows poor memory performance, it can be argued that this must have been due to more superficial processing. To properly test the theory, psychologists need to devise a method of measuring the depth and shallowness of memory processing that works independently of memory performance. Despite the lack of such a method, the levels of processing model is generally accepted by psychologists today.

The hippocampus is the area of the brain that sorts memories, deciding which ones are important enough to be stored in long-term memory.

hippocampus

The "software" of memory is its functional components and the processes it is capable of. The "hardware" is the central nervous system. Deep within our brains, memories are sorted in a region called the hippocampus. It acts as a gatekeeper, determining whether information is significant enough to pass into long-term storage. The hippocampus can also be described as the "printing press" for new memories. Important memories are "printed" by the hippocampus and filed away indefinitely in the cerebral cortex, which can be seen as the "library" for important memories.

Long-term memory

Information stored in the long-term memory can be divided into two types:

- *explicit memory:* this is consciously accessible and is also known as declarative memory;
- *implicit* or nondeclarative memory.

Explicit memory is usually divided into at least two types: episodic memory, which involves remembering particular events or specific episodes in your life; and semantic memory, which concerns the general knowledge that we acquire about the world. Implicit memory involves skills that we know but could not always describe, such as riding a bicycle, playing basketball, or typing. There seems to be general agreement that implicit memory is independent of explicit or consciously accessible memory.

Retrieval

Having encoded and stored information that has been processed by the senses, we then have to be able to effectively retrieve it from our filing system. What we are able to retrieve depends largely on the context in which the information was encoded or classified in the first place, and to what extent it matches the retrieval context. This is called the encoding specificity principle. For example, many of us have been embarrassed by our failure to recognize friends or acquaintances when we meet them in an unusual context.

There are two types of retrieval: recall and recognition. When investigating recall in an experimental context, researchers might present people with information, such as a story, during what is called the learning episode. The researchers then ask them to recall certain aspects of the story. Free recall is when people are asked to remember as much of the story as they can without any assistance. The "tip of the tongue phenomenon" mentioned earlier (*see* page 60)

Curriculum Context

Students should be able to describe the operation of long-term memory, and distinguish between implicit and explicit memory.

illustrates the nature of one common problem in free recall—we often have only partial access to information that we are trying to retrieve. Cued recall is when people are presented with a prompt (such as a category or the first letter of the word) to retrieve a certain piece of information. For example, they might be asked: "Tell me all the names of people beginning with 'J' who were in the story that I read to you yesterday." Cued recall tends to be easier for people than free recall. However, cues can also introduce distortion and bias.

Recognition is the easiest type of retrieval. Some of the actual memory material is presented, and you have to make a decision about it. "Forced-choice recognition" is when you are presented with, say, two items, only one of which you have seen previously. You are then asked to point out which of the two items you saw before. It is a forced choice in that you must choose one of the two items.

Experiments have indicated that two independent processes can contribute to recognition: context retrieval and familiarity. Context retrieval depends on explicit recollection of time and place. For example, you may recognize someone as the person you saw on the bus when you were coming home from college last Friday.

In familiarity recognition, you see someone who looks vaguely familiar. You know you have seen them before, but you cannot remember when or where. This type of recognition taps into a familiarity process, but there is no explicit recollection, so it is a less detailed form of recognition.

Physical and psychological influences on recall

Recall performance is influenced by your physical or psychological state. If you learn something when you are very calm and are tested when you are very excited,

your ability to recall information is reduced. But if you learn while calm and then are tested while calm, or learn while you are excited and then are tested while excited, you tend to perform better. This is known as state-dependent learning.

When either cued recall or recognition are tested, differences in state or context have less predictable effects. That is mainly because a certain amount of the information provided at learning and test is constant during recall and recognition tests. The potential for a mismatch between learning and remembering is substantially reduced. Also, the familiarity part of recognition does not depend on context, although the explicit recollection may be state-dependent.

Forgetting

Forgetting can be defined as the loss of information, due to interference or other blockage of retrieval. Forgetting may well occur not because of storage limitations, but because similar memories become confused and interfere with each other when we try to retrieve them. In order to understand better how memory works, we need to understand some of the factors that can influence the forgetting of information.

There are two traditional views of forgetting. One argues that memory fades or decays over time. The second view sees forgetting as a more active process. It occurs because memory traces are disrupted, obscured, or overlaid by other memories. In other words, forgetting happens because of interference. The consensus view is that both of these processes occur, but it is difficult to separate out the individual contributions of the two factors.

In experiments in 1975 and 1980 by D. R. Godden and Alan Baddeley, divers were asked to learn information in two contexts: on a beach and while diving. They were later asked to recall the information. The divers remembered far more if they recalled the information in the same context in which they learned it.

Our experiences undoubtedly interact in our memories and tend to run into one another. As a result, our memory of one experience is often related to our memory of another experience. The more similar two experiences, the greater the likelihood that they will interact in our memory. This can be helpful, since new learning can build on old. But if it is important to separate two memories of different occasions, interference can mean that we remember less accurately than we would like. For example, memories from two different birthdays might become confused with one another.

Curriculum Context

Students should be familiar with the primary findings of Ebbinghaus's nonsense-syllable studies or Bahrick's more recent research examining very long-term memory.

The Ebbinghaus tradition

The German experimental psychologist Hermann Ebbinghaus (1850–1909) is famous for his research into forgetting. In one experiment Ebbinghaus taught himself 169 separate lists of 13 nonsense syllables. He then relearned each list after an interval ranging from 21 minutes to 31 days. To test how much he had forgotten, he used a measure called the savings score (how long it took him to relearn the list).

Ebbinghaus found that his rate of forgetting was roughly exponential. This means that forgetting is rapid at first, then slows down. This observation has been shown to apply across a range of different materials and learning conditions. For instance, if you stop studying French when you leave school, your vocabulary declines rapidly over the next 12 months. After this, the rate at which you forget vocabulary gradually slows, and you eventually reach a plateau where your knowledge stays the same. If you study French again five to ten years later, you might be surprised at how much vocabulary you have retained. Also, although you have forgotten some of your French vocabulary, you can relearn it much faster than someone who has never learned French.

The Bartlett tradition

The work of psychologist Sir Frederick Bartlett exemplifies the second great tradition in memory research. In his book *Remembering* (1932), Bartlett attacked the Ebbinghaus tradition. He argued that the study of nonsense syllables does not tell us much about the way memory operates in the real world. Bartlett focused on meaningful materials remembered under relatively natural conditions.

In some of Bartlett's studies, subjects were asked to read a story to themselves then recall it later. He found that people recalled the story in their own way, but also found some general trends:

- The stories tended to become shorter.
- People made sense of unfamiliar material by changing it to fit their preexisting ideas and cultural expectations.
- The changes people made matched the reactions and emotions that they had experienced when they first heard the story.

Curriculum Context

Students may find it useful to compare the findings of Ebbinghaus and Bartlett.

The War of The Ghosts

Bartlett used two basic methods in his experiments: serial reproduction and repeated reproduction. Serial reproduction is similar to the game "Chinese Whispers." One person passes some information to a second person, who passes the same information to a third, and so on. The "story" that reaches the final person in the group is then compared with the original. Repeated reproduction is when someone is asked to repeat the same piece of information at certain intervals—from 15 minutes to a few years—after first learning it.

Bartlett's most famous experiment used a North American folktale called "The War of the Ghosts." He chose the story because it did not relate to the English culture of his subjects (Cambridge students). The subjects were asked to memorize the story, then retell it later. In the retellings, the students altered the story to sound much more like English tales.

Bartlett concluded that people tend to rationalize material—they turn it into something they feel more comfortable with and find easier to understand. According to Bartlett, remembering is an imaginative reconstruction from a whole active mass of organized past reactions or experiences. It is, therefore, hardly ever really exact, even in the most basic cases of rote recapitulation.

Bartlett argued that what people remember is to some extent driven by their emotional and personal commitment to—and investment in—the original event. The memory system retains "a little outstanding detail," and the remainder is an elaboration or a reconstruction based on the original event. Bartlett referred to this as the "reconstructive," as opposed to the "reproductive," nature of memory.

Organization and errors

In the 1960s and 1970s researchers carried out studies to discover how well chess players could remember the positions of the pieces on a board. The studies showed that chess masters could remember 95 percent of the positions after a single five-second glance. Weaker chess players were able to position only 40 percent of the pieces correctly and needed eight attempts to reach 95 percent accuracy. These findings suggest that the advantage enjoyed by the chess masters stemmed from their ability to perceive the chessboard as an organized whole, rather than as a collection of individual pieces. Experiments in which expert bridge players were asked to recall bridge hands and electronics experts were asked to remember electronic circuits produced similar results. In each case it appears that experts are able to organize the material into a coherent and meaningful pattern that results in significant enhancement to their memory.

We have already seen that organizing information at the time of retrieval (in the form of cueing) can aid recall. However, these studies revealed the benefits of organization at the time of learning.

Most people have a poor memory for many aspects of their daily life. If a piece of information is not useful in everyday life, then it is unlikely that we will successfully remember it. For instance, can you remember whether the head on a coin in your pocket faces to the left or

Curriculum Context

It might be interesting to test your own and your classmates' ability to memorize the position of pieces on a chessboard.

the right? Generally speaking, people are very bad at answering this question correctly, despite using the coins almost every day. Errors can be caused by a number of factors, including inattention, which leads to incomplete encoding, and initial misunderstanding. Hypnosis or memory-producing drugs do not improve the accuracy of recall.

Memory and crime

Considerable weight is still placed on eyewitness testimony by the legal profession, the police, and the press. Eyewitnesses may be expected to recall an event with a level of detail that is quite unrealistic in the context of what we know about the way our memories work. Eyewitness reports of crimes may also depend on the witness's emotional investment and their personal perspective. They may, for example, be more sympathetic toward the victim of the crime than toward the perpetrator.

Curriculum Context

Students might be asked to hypothesize about the role of reconstructive memory processes in cases of eyewitness testimony.

In a crime many factors can combine to make eyewitness reports unreliable:

- When people experience extreme stress, their attention can be narrowed in focus, which means that their perception is often biased.

Mistaken Identity

The Australian psychologist Donald Thompson took part in a television debate on the subject of eyewitness testimony. He was very active in arguing for the unreliability of eyewitness evidence. Some time later the police arrested him but refused to explain why. When a woman picked him out of a lineup at the police station, he discovered he was to be charged with rape.

When he asked for further details, it became clear that the rape had been committed while he was taking part in the television discussion. Obviously, he then had a very good alibi—a police officer had taken part in the same discussion. It turned out that the woman had been raped in a room where the program was on the television. This was an instance of what is known as transference of memory. The woman's memory of the rapist had been "contaminated" by the face she saw on the television during the rape.

- People tend to remember less accurately in a violent situation.
- A weapon at the scene can distract attention from the perpetrator of the crime.
- People are much better at recognizing faces than recalling other information, but clothing is a powerful source of bias in recognition. Someone wearing clothing similar to that of the criminal could be incorrectly identified as the criminal.
- People tend to be poorer at recognizing the faces of individuals from racial and ethnic groups other than their own. This phenomenon does not seem to be related to racial prejudice.

Another powerful influence in the distortion of memory is the use of leading questions—making assumptions or implying what happened. "Did you see the man who raped the woman?" is an example of a leading question, since it assumes that a rape has taken place. It can result in far more confirmations of an alleged crime than a question such as "Did you see a man rape the woman?"

A central message of these studies is that memory is not a passive process. People do not just receive information and store it in their memory; they impose meaning on that information, molding memories to make them consistent with their world view.

Influencing memory

In laboratory experiments in the mid-1970s Elizabeth Loftus found that people respond just as rapidly and confidently to leading or misleading questions as they do to questions phrased without bias. Even if participants notice that new information has been introduced, it can still become part of their memory. Memory bias, therefore, can be introduced retrospectively. In one experiment in 1974 Loftus and her colleague John Palmer asked groups of students to watch a series of films, each showing a traffic accident.

Afterward they had to answer questions about what had happened. One of the questions was, "How fast were the cars going when they ------ each other?" The gap was filled with a different word for each group of students. The words used were "smashed," "collided," "bumped," "hit," and "contacted."

The researchers found that students' estimates of the cars' speeds were influenced by the choice of verb in the question. They concluded that the students' memory of the accident had been altered by the implied information given in the question.

A year later Loftus carried out another experiment in which she again showed participants a film of a traffic accident. This time she asked some of the students, "How fast was the white sports car going when it passed the barn while traveling along the country road?" There was no barn in the film. A week later those who had been asked this question were more likely to say they remembered seeing a barn. Even if participants were asked simply, "Did you see a barn?" they were more likely a week later to "remember" seeing it. Loftus concluded that the actual memory can be changed by the introduction of misleading information.

The findings of Loftus and colleagues have great significance for police interviewing techniques, as well

Memories of a traffic accident can be influenced by the questions that eyewitnesses are asked. For example, if witnesses are asked whether a truck hit the signpost, they will "insert" a signpost into their original memory even if they did not actually see one.

as very controversial implications for events associated with possible child abuse. Are people in therapy recovering genuine memories of what happened during their childhood, or are they being induced or misled by the therapist's suggestions to remember things that did not really happen?

Improving memory

It is easy to damage the neural systems underlying memory, for example through alcohol or drug abuse. It is more difficult to enhance our neural "hardware". The only way to improve memory is to make sure that the "software" running on these neural systems is working at its best.

When Ebbinghaus was learning his nonsense syllables, he found that there was a direct relationship between the number of learning trials and the amount of syllables he was able to retain. Ebbinghaus concluded that the amount learned depended simply on the time spent learning. If you doubled the amount of time spent learning, you would double the amount of information stored. This is the basic relationship underlying all literature on human learning.

Today people have access to numerous electronic gadgets that act as memory aids. They include computers, personal organizers, and voice recorders.

Ebbinghaus also noted that it is better to distribute learning trials across an extended period rather than to mass them together in a single block. Little and often is the key principle here. Cramming for an examination cannot replace solid, sustained study.

Motivation to learn information is another important factor, although its effect may well be indirect. It influences the amount of time spent attending to the material to be learned, and that affects the amount of learning taking place.

The way in which we process information is crucial. People seek meaning in information they are trying to remember. If there is an absence of meaning, they try to impose their own. A general rule is that it often helps to relate new material to yourself and to your circumstances as richly and elaborately as possible.

There is a complex, mutually reinforcing relationship between attention, interest, expertise, and memory. The more expert you become in a particular field, the more interest you will have in it, and those two aspects will reinforce each other in improving your memory for material in that field.

Mnemonics

People with so-called "exceptional memories" often use mnemonics. A mnemonic is a visual or verbal method of organizing information to make it easier to remember. The two most popular visual mnemonics are the "method of loci" and "peg words."

Curriculum Context

Students should be able to describe strategies for improving memory, such as developing and describing mnemonic devices to help learn psychological concepts.

The method of loci (loci is Latin for "places") is said to have been devised by the Greek poet Simonides in about 500 BC. He was said to have devised a technique of visualizing a room or building in great detail and then imagining various to-be-remembered objects or pieces of information in particular locations. Whenever Simonides needed to remember what these items were, he would imagine himself walking through the room or building and "picking up" those pieces of information. The technique seems to work particularly well with concrete words, such as names of objects. But it can also work with abstract words, provided you can come up with a representative image of the abstract concept and locate it appropriately.

Peg words help you remember lists of items. Each number is assigned a word: 1 is a bun, 2 is a shoe, 3 is a tree, 4 is a door, 5 is a hive, 6 is sticks, 7 is heaven, 8 is a gate, 9 is wine, 10 is a hen. If the first word on your list is cat, you link this image with the number 1, bun. So you might create a visual image of a cat eating a bun. If the second word is dog, you might think of a dog chewing a shoe, or even a dog wearing a shoe—generally speaking, the more bizarre the image, the better this technique seems to work.

Classical mnemonics relied mainly on visual imagery. In later times, verbal mnemonics were developed. These tend to fall into one of two categories: either a reduction code or an elaboration code. A reduction code reduces the amount of information. For example, to remember certain rules of trigonometry, schoolchildren were once taught to use the nonsense word SOHCAHTOA. By contrast, an elaboration code increases the information. Another way to learn the same trigonometric relationships, is to use the expression Some Old Horses Chew Apples Heartily Throughout Old Age. In each case the coding technique produces information that is easier to remember because it is more meaningful to the user.

Memory development

Memory development can be seen as the gradual emergence of more complex strategies for encoding and retrieving memories. As children begin to use language, they start to use linguistic labels to encode materials more richly and as cues when retrieving items. Children also develop a better awareness of how good or poor their memory is in particular situations, and how likely they are to be able to remember certain pieces of information. Studies of implicit memory indicate that it may be present in its full form in children as young as three years.

What underlies memory development is not yet known. A child's knowledge and language ability are undoubtedly important, but biological factors are likely

Curriculum Context

Students might be asked to illustrate developmental changes in physical, cognitive, and social development from the prenatal period throughout the life span.

to be central, too. Hardly anyone can reliably remember information from before the age of about four years, although it is a time when experience is at its richest. One explanation for this could be that memories of experiences before the age of four may well exist, but in a form that no longer allows the individual to access them. This may be due to differences in the way in which young children and adults encode their memories.

Aging and memory

Given the progressive increase in the average age of the population in the majority of Western countries, it is important to identify memory changes that can truly be attributed to aging. Studies of aging and memory have produced some consistent findings. Working memory seems to remain quite efficient over the years, but tasks requiring working memory become more difficult. If people are shown a sequence of digits and asked to repeat them in reverse order, for example, older participants are less apt to do well than younger ones. But old and young perform equally well when asked to repeat a sequence of digits in the same order in which they were shown.

Long-term memory performance declines significantly with age, especially in situations requiring free recall. Recognition holds up well, but it becomes more familiarity based. When recognition demands contextual memory, deficits do emerge with age. This may mean that old people are more susceptible to suggestion and bias in their memory.

Implicit memory is usually tested by evaluating behavior rather than recollection of the memory experience. Results show it not only matures early in children, but also holds up well in old age. Aging also has little effect on semantic memory, which seems to

By the time children begin to take tests they have developed memory skills and an awareness of how good their memory is in different situations.

improve throughout life. Evidence suggests that age-related memory loss arises partly because the frontal lobes deteriorate relatively early. Prospective memory (remembering to do something in the future) has been linked to the frontal brain functions.

Brain damage

One area of considerable interest to researchers is whether changes in memory due to "normal" aging are actually signs of brain damage. For example, "mild cognitive impairment" has been defined as a category lying between normal aging and full-blown dementia. A lot of people diagnosed with this condition slip into full-blown dementia within five years. Memory dysfunction is typically an early hallmark of dementia. This is particularly the case in the most common form of dementia, senile dementia of the Alzheimer type. In the early stages of the illness only memory is affected, but later on many other capacities can be impaired, such as perception, language, and executive or frontal lobe functions. Unlike people suffering from more selective forms of amnesia, patients with Alzeimer's disease appear to be deficient on tests of implicit as well as explicit memory.

Amnesiacs

The "amnesiac syndrome" is the purest example of memory impairment and involves some form of specific brain injury. The damage usually involves two key areas of the forebrain: the hippocampus and the diencephalon. Patients exhibit severe anterograde amnesia and a degree of retrograde amnesia.

Generally, patients with amnesia have normal intelligence, language ability, and immediate memory span. It is their long-term memory that is impaired. Amnesiacs may be unable to learn new information over a substantial time span, although they can typically recite back information within their attention

---

Alzheimer's disease

An incurable disease that causes loss of memory and other cognitive skills later in life.

Anterograde amnesia

Inability to create memories after the episode that caused the amnesia.

Retrograde amnesia

Inability to remember memories from before the episode that caused the amnesia.

span; they may well retain childhood memories but find it almost impossible to acquire new ones; they may remember how to tell the time, but not know what year it is; they may readily learn new skills like typing, but then deny ever having used a keyboard. It seems then that it is the "printing press" of long-term memory (located in the hippocampus or diencephalon) rather than the "library" (located in the cerebral cortex) that is damaged in amnesiac individuals.

Psychological damage

Some psychologists believe that some memory disorders are caused by psychological or emotional factors rather than neurological brain injury. For example, there are instances of individuals entering a dissociative state in which they seem to become partly or totally separated from their memories. An example is the fugue state, when someone completely loses track of their personal identity and the memories that went with it. They are usually unaware that anything is wrong and will often adopt a new identity. The fugue only becomes apparent when the patient "comes to" days, months, or even years after the precipitating event. Another form of dissociative state defined by some psychologists is multiple personality disorder, in which a number of personalities apparently emerge to handle different aspects of an individual's past life. This serves to protect the individual from potentially harmful memories and can be connected with crime. An example is the 1977 Los Angeles case of Kenneth Bianchi. He was charged with the rape and murder of several women. Despite strong evidence against him, he denied his guilt and claimed that he knew nothing about the murders. Under hypnosis another personality called Steve emerged, who claimed responsibility for the rapes and murders. When removed from the hypnotic trance, Bianchi claimed to remember nothing of the conversation between Steve and the hypnotist.

Diencephalon

A group of structures right in the center of the brain. For memory, the most important are the thalamus and the maxillary bodies.

Language Processing

Some psycholinguists have suggested that people are born with a predisposition to acquire language. Over time the main focus of the study of language has moved from its philosophical meaning, through cognitive and perceptual models of language processing, to investigations of the relationship between language and the brain.

Language is the most powerful communication tool people possess. Through language we communicate not only ideas and feelings but also culture, ways of life, and world views. The faculty of language is common to all people, but at the same time we have many different languages, dialects, or accents.

Language in nonhuman species

Many nonhuman species possess powerful ways of communicating information within their group. Insects, for example, release chemicals called pheromones that allow them to communicate with other members of the same species. Honeybees also use body language to communicate. They perform complex dances to let other bees know the location of a new source of food and how much food there is.

Some of the most intriguing research into animal languages has involved chimpanzees. Chimps cannot speak because they lack the necessary voice organs, but it has proved possible to teach them sign language. Washoe, the first chimpanzee to be involved in language-acquisition experiments in the 1960s, learned 132 manual signs in four years. She was capable of putting several signs together to make a few meaningful phrases, (for example, "more fruit," "Washoe sorry").

Another famous chimpanzee, Sarah, could arrange symbols on a magnetic board to form short sentences like "Sarah insert apple in dish." She was also able to produce new meanings by substituting one word for another in a given sentence.

Many scientists do not think that the evidence of chimpanzee communication shows that animals have language skills comparable to those of people. Chimps' language behavior might be the product of sophisticated imitation rather than true linguistic processing. Chimps do not develop language spontaneously, and when taught they do not show a great creativity in their productions. Also, chimps learn slowly, need careful training, and are inflexible in the way they give responses.

Syntax

An important feature of language is the way that words work together. For example, in English we can combine the words "Mary," "Paul," and "pushes" in two different ways, with different meanings: "Mary pushes Paul" and "Paul pushes Mary." The sentences contain the same words, but the word order is different. The associations between a specific word order and a meaning are governed by rules. This is known as syntax. With each rule we can create an infinite number of sentences simply by replacing the words in a sentence with other words (for example, "John pushes Bill," "Bill watches Mary").

A syntactic structure tree applied to the sentence "The actor entered the room." The whole unit is a sentence. Within that the noun phrases are "The actor" and the "the room," and the verb phrase is "entered the room." The sentence can be further broken down into individual words that are either determiners, nouns, and verbs.

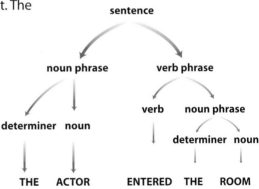

The structure of language

Sentences have a critical role in language because they allow us to express whole ideas and thoughts. They convey meaningful data, otherwise known as semantic information. Sentences are made of words organized in a way that is defined by syntactic rules. Words themselves are composed of morphemes. A morpheme is the smallest linguistic unit that conveys meaning. For example, the word "blueish" is made of two morphemes, "blue" and "ish."

Phonemes are the speech sounds that words are made of. Each phoneme is represented by a conventional symbol. For example, the word "bat" is made of three phonemes: /b/, /æ/, and /t/. Each language has a different set of phonemes. Some are common to many languages (such as, /b/, /p/, /t/), while others are specific to only a few (such as the click sounds of the Khoisan languages spoken in southern Africa).

Although we can represent a word by a string of phonemes (such as, /kritik/ for the word "critic"), it is customary to group phonemes into syllables (such as, /kri·tik/). Syllables are important in language processing because they probably play a central role in speech production and perception.

Language is more than just phonemes, syllables, words, and sentences. Rhythm, intonation, and speed matter, too. Such features, termed suprasegmentals, carry a lot of meaning. The sentence "I like jello" means something different if we put the emphasis on "I" (I like jello more than my neighbor does) or "like" (I like jello as opposed

Noam Chomsky: Predisposed to Learn Language

One of the most influential advocates of the importance of syntax in language is U.S. linguist Noam Chomsky. Chomsky claimed that verbal communication is so complex, and yet learned so easily by children, that people must be born with the predisposition to understand and use rule-based communication. He argues that the linguistic environment to which children are exposed in their early years is simply not rich enough for them to learn the complexities of language. Chomsky says that we are born with some sort of Language Acquisition Device, or an inbuilt Universal Grammar, which gives us a head start when learning a language. Chimpanzees and other nonhuman animals probably do not possess such inbuilt capacity.

to disliking it). An important type of information is prosody, which in this context means the melody and stress structure of speech.

Language and the brain

Scientific knowledge of the relationship between language and the brain comes from two sources: neuropsychological studies of people with brain injury who show language impairments, and brain-imaging studies, in which brain activity in healthy individuals is monitored while they are engaged in language processing.

A radio announcer talking into a microphone. His words consist of phonemes, or speech sounds. The rules governing how phonemes are used are called phonotactic rules. Sentences and words can be broken down into morphemes—a morpheme is the smallest meaningful linguistic unit.

Aphasia is the most common language disorder caused by brain damage. The first cases of aphasia were observed by pathologist Paul Broca. Nonfluent aphasia is a type of aphasia characterized by slow, laborious speech. It is typically caused by brain damage in a specific region of the brain—the motor association cortex in the left frontal lobe (Broca's area). About a quarter of all penetrating head injuries lead to aphasia.

Lesions farther back from Broca's area have a different effect on speech. Damage to areas in the left temporal (front) and parietal (middle) lobes generally causes receptive aphasia or Wernicke's aphasia, named for German neurologist Carl Wernicke. This condition is characterized by serious difficulty understanding speech, although speech production remains fairly fluent. Thus, contrary to nonfluent aphasics, receptive aphasics do not understand when they are spoken to, but they answer anyway—in a voluble and often irrelevant manner.

Not all lesions in the so-called language areas lead to a language impairment. Conversely, language

Curriculum Context

Students should recognize that specific functions are centered in specific lobes of the cerebral cortex.

impairments can sometimes originate from "nonlanguage" areas. On the whole, however, neuropsychological studies strongly support the view that the language faculty is localized in particular parts of the brain. Neuroimaging (brain imaging) also indicates that the left hemisphere participates in linguistic tasks more actively than the right. Moreover, distinct brain regions are activated during language processing. However, a problem is that the region apparently activated by a specific type of language processing can vary from one study to another. This could be because not all studies use the same stimuli or pose the same task.

In sum, it would appear that if there is such a thing as a language device in the brain, it is probably located in the left hemisphere and only humans possess it. Nevertheless, it is unlikely that specific language abilities are controlled by brain areas entirely independently of each other and dedicated to one task alone. There is a considerable overlap in brain activity across linguistic tasks.

Language comprehension

Understanding spoken language is fast and automatic. Every day we hear thousands of words and sentences, and usually make sense of them immediately. However, effortless as it may seem, recognizing speech involves a great deal of knowledge about sounds, words, and grammatical rules, together with fine-tuned hearing and processing skills.

Curriculum Context

Students should be familiar with the role of grammar in language systems.

The entire act of comprehending speech begins with the perception of air-pressure changes (the acoustic signal) and ends with the total integration of the message. At the start of language processing our perceptual system has to interpret the acoustic signal as a string of phonemes. But mapping the acoustic signal onto the 40 or so English phonemes is more complicated than it seems. The listener must deal with the fact that phonemes do not have their own "acoustic signature." For example, the phoneme /s/ is acoustically different in "sue" and "see" because it is modified by the following vowel.

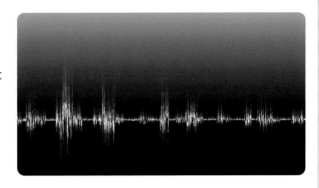

Once the acoustic signal has been interpreted as a string of phonemes, lexical access can begin. Lexical access is the process of matching a string of phonemes to various possible words. However, in actual speech there are few clear pauses between words. So lexical access must operate along with a process known as word segmentation. Research shows that listeners use different types of information to locate word boundaries in the signal. They include sense, pronunciation, stress, and pauses. Generally, we prefer segmentation solutions that yield real words and meaningful sentences.

Next, the listener needs to make sense of the words' individual meanings in the context of the sentence. A

The vibrations of the voice cause changes in air pressure that are recorded. Each phoneme, or linguistic unit, is represented by a different pattern.

Discourse Processing

In the 1990s psychologist Walter Kintsch proposed a discourse-processing theory that first involves condensing a story to a few propositions such as "It's six o'clock," "The lady needs bread," "She goes to the bakery," "The bakery is on a popular street," "The lady has an argument with the baker," and so on. The propositions are stored in short-term memory and then completed by top-down information retrieved from long-term memory. For example, we know that stores on popular streets stay open late, which is why the bakery is open at six o'clock. In the end, the integration of propositions (bottom-up) and inferences drawn from long-term memory (top-down) results in a streamlined representation of the discourse in which most of the details have been lost.

crucial step in sentence comprehension is parsing. Parsing involves taking account of word order and other information to decide which word is the subject of the sentence, which is the object, and so on. This is the stage at which we become aware of the difference between "The dog chases the cat" and "The cat chases the dog."

When sentences are assembled into discourse (or a logical sequence of events), they create rich messages that contain several major ideas. However, our memory capacity does not allow us to remember all the words of the discourse. Instead, we can extract only key words and ideas. The way that we do this is known as discourse processing.

Reading

Like speech comprehension, reading involves a series of well-orchestrated processes. Readers must recognize written symbols as letters, group them into words, look them up in their mental lexicon, and access their meaning. Further processes involve using syntactical rules to make sense of sentences and drawing inferences from long-term memory to comprehend the text as a whole.

Children learning to read are not aware of the complex processes involved, even at a very basic level of reading ability.

Many processes are common to both spoken and written language recognition. However, the two activities differ in important ways. The major difference is how the information reaches our senses. While the auditory signal is transitory, written words remain visible. This difference has consequences for the type of perceptual mechanisms used in reading. For example, our eyes can jump back to earlier words if needed.

Another fundamental difference is that speech and comprehension and production come naturally to the young learner, while reading and writing are the result of long, formal, and effortful training. Finally, unlike speech, written sentences have clear boundaries between words. So word segmentation, which is so critical in speech processing, is not an issue in reading.

Language acquisition

Whatever their talent, motivation, or personality, children in every part of the world easily acquire language. In a mere four or five years after they are born, children manage to learn the speech sounds, vocabulary, syntactical rules, and communicative skills of their own particular environment.

One of the most intriguing questions is how children learn language so easily. People often contend that humans must be born equipped to learn language. But at the same time, exposure to language through parents or siblings seems necessary as well. Indeed, children who are deprived of language exposure during their early years are rarely able to master language as fully as infants who are raised in a normal linguistic environment.

Language acquisition occurs in various stages. These stages generally follow a typical timetable that starts from the moment of birth, or possibly in the womb.

The first 12 months

Despite the fact that infants rarely talk before at least eight months, familiarization with speech sounds is well on its way before that age. For example, soon after birth, if presented with a choice of English or French, American infants will tend to listen longer to English and French infants to French. This indicates that exposure to the mother's voice during the last months of pregnancy has familiarized infants with their native language.

At the phonemic level young infants show impressive perceptual capacities as well. For example, they can discriminate critical phonetic contrasts, such as that between /ba/ and /pa/. This is quite an accomplishment given how similar the two syllables sound. Infants can also distinguish some sounds that are not encountered in their own language. For instance, in Japanese the difference between /l/ and /r/ does not exist. Adult Japanese speakers have difficulty distinguishing between these two sounds, but very young Japanese infants do not have this problem.

A fetus can hear some sounds in the womb, so language development can begin before an infant is even born. Recent studies also show that for up to a year after birth, babies exhibit a preference for a piece of music played repeatedly during pregnancy.

No matter how good they are at perceiving fine speech contrasts and remembering them, infants younger than six months do not generally understand words. They may be able to say a few very frequent words such as their own first name and "mommy" and "daddy," but the semantic level of their linguistic system is still relatively undeveloped.

The hypersensitivity to phonetic contrasts that characterizes the first six months disappears between six months and a year, during which period infants' perceptual capacities narrow down to only those phonetic contrasts that are relevant to their own language. Although actual talking emerges mostly during the second year of life, babbling is often present before one year: the first vowel is /a/, the first consonants /p/ and /b/. Infants may even produce a few words as early as eight months. Early vocabulary tends to refer to concrete things that can move around, such as "ball" and "car".

Age one and beyond

During the second year of life the infant's language system grows rapidly in complexity and efficiency. Speech perception capacities are now better attuned to segmenting speech. Syntax is falling in place as well, as infants start grasping important notions such as the past tense of verbs and the composite nature of sentences.

Most noticeable is the child's growing verbal activity. However, most of the sentences they produce are only one word long. At this stage children might use a single word to mean different things. For example, they may use the word "ball" to mean anything that is round, anything that rolls, or any toy. Or they may assign a word to a specific instance of that word (for example, "ball" refers only to a ball in the neighbor's backyard). This problem of appropriate syntax disappears quickly as the child is exposed to multiple examples of a word in various contexts.

An infant's second birthday usually corresponds to a dramatic acceleration in language acquisition. The child's vocabulary expands from a few dozen words at around 18 months to several thousand words by age five. At the same time, the one-word stage gives way to the two-word stage, a telegraphic (fragmented) style that precedes the emergence of real sentences.

Curriculum Context

Estimates of the average vocabulary of an adult range from about 40,000 to about 60,000 words.

Children produce their first real sentences, which contain verbs and function words, as early as two and a half years. This stage is central to language acquisition because it implies that children start to have a handle on syntactical rules. In fact, they master some of them so well that they sometimes use them inappropriately, adding, for example, the –ed suffix to all verbs in the past tense (such as "holded" for "held").

The problem of syntactical overgeneralization gradually disappears as children come to realize that, alongside rules, there are exceptions. By age four or five, children's language knowledge is often described as comparable to adults' in quality.

Children from any part of the world go through the same sequence of language development regardless of the amount of exposure to language (as long as there is at least some); so do children deprived of hearing or sight. This suggests there is an innate machinery for language that works despite wide variations in the environment. However, this machinery has constraints, too. For example, there seems to be a critical period in early life when language acquisition is easy. After this period language acquisition becomes much more difficult or even impossible. A separate critical period occurs at around puberty, at 12 to 14 years of age. During this phase, language skills can be reallocated as necessary to different parts of the brain. This property is known as neural plasticity. Learning foreign languages before puberty is therefore much less effortful, and brain injuries affecting language areas can be overcome.

Cape Verdeans speak a creole language. A pidgin is a roughly made new language, with little grammar or syntax. A creole is a full-blown language developed from a pidgin. It is usually invented by children who are exposed to the pidgin. Only children have the ability to create new rules of syntax for a language. In later life we lose this ability.

The idea that people are born with a predisposition to learn language is supported by the observation that the linguistic input received by infants is often quite poor or incomplete. This is termed the poverty of input hypothesis. For instance, the speech that infants hear contains hesitations, false starts, unfinished sentences, mumbled words, and even ungrammatical forms. Moreover, children are not normally exposed to enough examples of grammatical constructions to extrapolate the correct grammar. Yet, people still learn the subtleties of language within a few years.

Wild and isolated children

The importance of social factors in language acquisition is illustrated most dramatically in cases of total deprivation of social interaction during the first years of life. Wild children, abandoned in forests and found alive years later, provide a demonstration of how critical exposure to normal socialization is. Ramu, a young boy discovered in India in 1976, was apparently raised by wolves. He learned to bathe and dress himself, but he never learned to speak. Among the other 30 or so reported wild children the patterns of behavior were all very similar. Although some eventually managed to speak a few words, none ever learned language to a normal level.

Isolated children are individuals who were raised by people, but under extreme social and physical conditions. Genie was discovered in 1970 at the age of 14. From about 20 months she had been tied to a chair and denied normal socialization. When she was found, she had no language. Great efforts were made to teach her to speak. She was able to acquire some language (for example, "no more take wax," "another house have dog"), but could not form proper sentences.

Another isolated child, Isabelle, who was hidden away during infancy and found when she was six, learned to speak within a year. Her speech was as good as that of her classmates. Rehabilitation was almost perfect because Isabelle was exposed to language before she reached puberty.

Curriculum Context

Students should be able to use case studies such as Genie or the Wild Boy of Aveyron to examine language development.

Problem Solving

The psychology of problem solving encompasses the processes that lead us to all kinds of everyday decision making and the way we estimate probability. Problem solving is in this sense distinct from reasoning, which involves discernment and judgment. The study of problem solving also examines the nature of creativity.

Curriculum Context

Students should be able to identify problem solving as a directed and productive example of thinking.

How do people solve problems? What makes some problems harder to solve than others? Can creativity be examined scientifically? Modern psychologists regard problem solving as a search process in which solvers use their mental faculties to find a path that leads to a goal. The route may be preplanned or found by chance; the ultimate objective may be identified from the start or stumbled on along the way. The methods used to explore problem solving cast fascinating light on the functioning of the human mind.

Trial and error

One of the simplest and most widely used methods of problem solving is trial and error. It is a process in which lots of possible solutions are tested, usually in a rather random fashion, until the right answer is found. U.S. psychologist Edward Lee Thorndike studied this type of problem solving in cats. He observed that cats used trial and error methods to find their way out of a closed box. The behavior of cats in such situations casts interesting light on that of humans, who are most likely to use trial and error when the way to solve a problem directly is not obvious.

Curriculum Context

Students might be asked to provide examples of how insight is used in problem solving.

Insight

Trial-and-error learning differs from insight, which requires a leap of intuition for the solution to be identified. German Gestalt psychologist Wolfgang Köhler studied problem solving through insight by examining the ability of apes to reach bananas placed

just beyond their grasp above or outside their cage. To get hold of the fruit, the apes had to stick two sticks together or move a box so that they could stand on it. It seemed that solutions to the problem would come suddenly to the apes after a period of inactivity and reflection.

Insight is sometimes regarded as a higher form of problem solving than trial and error. In humans, however, the two methods are often complementary—the solution of most problems seems to involve a mixture of trial and error and insight. Psychologists have generally been more interested in insight, in which the solution seems to pop up out of nowhere. This seems to be particularly important in creative problem solving.

U.S. psychologist Edward Lee Thorndike studied problem solving in cats. He found that the cats used a trial-and-error strategy to solve the problem of getting out of a closed box. They were not able to use insight to solve the problem.

Functional fixity

Problems can be divided into several categories. First are "problems of arrangement" in which various objects need to be shuffled into some other form. One example is jigsaw puzzles; another is finding solutions to anagrams, such as: "What fruit is made up of the letters ENRAOG?" Psychologist N. R. F. Maier conducted one of the classic studies of arrangement problems in 1931. He placed a person in a room containing various objects, including a pair of pliers. There were also two strings hanging from the ceiling. The problem was to find a way of tying the two pieces of string together. The strings were placed so far apart that it was not possible to grab one piece, hold it, and walk over to the other piece of string. The hoped for solution was to tie the pliers to the end of one string and hold the first string. The additional weight of the pliers made the string behave as a pendulum. Thus it became possible

Curriculum Context

Curricula may ask students to analyze the obstacles that inhibit problem solving and decision-making.

to get hold of both bits of string and tie them together. Most of the people who took part in this experiment were unable to find the correct solution.

Experiments such as Maier's suggest that people find it hard to see how familiar objects can be used for unfamiliar purposes. Pliers are used normally to pull nails out of wood. This can make it difficult to see what else they might be used for. This effect is known as "functional fixity" or "functional fixedness."

A River-Crossing Problem

Suppose you are standing on one side of a river with a hen, a sack of corn, and a cat. You also have a boat. You want to carry all the items over to the other side of the river, but the boat is quite small and will carry only you and one other item across the river. You cannot leave the hen alone with the corn, or the cat alone with the hen. How can you move all the items over to the other side of the river in the shortest number of trips?

The solution is as follows. First, carry the hen to the other side of the river, then return. Next, take the corn to the other side of the river and return with the hen. Then, take the cat to the other side of the river, and leave it there with the sack of corn. Finally, return and take over the hen.

Problems such as this can be made more difficult by increasing the number of hens and cats.

Problems of transformation
Problems of transformation involve changing one state into another through the application of a set of rules. For instance, some psychologists have studied various "river-crossing problems" (*see* box above).

Curriculum Context

Students may be asked to describe different strategies involved in problem solving and decision making.

Solving this kind of problem involves making choices. One logical route to a solution is to use a problem-solving technique called the "state-space". It is a mathematical representation of the possibilities or states for a problem. Solving the problem involves finding the shortest possible pathway through the space. Because several different choices can be made at every step, the number of possible routes to solving the problem quickly becomes very large: for complex problems the number is astronomical. The classic example of this is chess. When deciding what move to make at a given point in a game, one strategy would be for a player to work out all the possible consequences of each move. In chess there are 20 possible opening moves. However, for subsequent moves the number of possibilities quickly becomes enormous. It is simply not feasible to calculate all the consequences of any move. If there were no shortcuts, the game of chess would never have been invented.

In chess there are 20 possible opening moves. In later stages there are about 30 legal moves from each position. On this basis, information theorist Claude Shannon calculated that in a typical game there are a total of 10^{120} possible moves—more than all the atoms in the Universe.

Means-end analysis

For complex problems we must have a strategy that prevents us from having to examine every possible path through the problem space. One of the most widely used approaches is known as means-end analysis. In the 1950s American psychologists Allen Newell and Herbert Simon tried to formulate a generalized set of strategies that could be applied to many different problems of means-end analysis. For example, imagine the case of trying to figure out how to travel from your house in New York to a friend's house in London, England. You might have a set of rules to follow, such as these:

- If the distance is less than 1 mile, walk.
- If the distance is between 1 and 5 miles, take a bus.
- If the distance is between 5 and 100 miles, take a train.
- If the distance to be traveled is greater than 100 miles, take an airplane.

Because the distance to be traveled is greater than 100 miles, the first rule that would be applied states "catch an airplane." However, there may be further conditions, termed enabling conditions, that need to be satisfied. In this case, one condition might be "get to the airport." You now have a new problem to solve. This is known as a subgoal. Suppose the airport is 3 miles from your home. You can then apply the second rule (take a bus) to help you get to the airport. Having gotten to the airport, you can then catch the flight to London.

Means-end analysis was seen originally as a problem-solving strategy that could be used in any situation. Indeed, the prototype model developed by Newell and Simon was known as the General Problem Solver (GPS). It was based on the assumption that human thought processes are comparable to the functioning of digital computers. However, this analogy, like so many others in the field of cognition, was only good so far. For example, when psychologists examined the performance of people who are very skilled in one particular field (such as chess players), they usually found that their expertise was restricted to a particular area. It was not transferable or more widely applicable to other areas. These people's problem-solving skills therefore do not arise from the application of some general-purpose strategy.

Making analogies

Another way of solving problems is by comparing them with similar instances—this is known as using analogies. Some experiments have shown that solutions may be found more easily if suitable analogies are suggested. However, it is much easier to see the value of analogies than to find the right one at the perfect moment. People tend to choose analogies that resemble the problem superficially—if, for example, the problem involves water, they come up with the other facts they know about liquids. These may or may not be relevant to the matter at hand.

General Problem Solver (GPS)

A computer program developed by Allen Newell, Herbert Simon, and J.C. Shaw that was designed to solve puzzles and problems. However the program had no learning capability and its intelligence was only second-hand.

Creativity

Creativity is a form of problem solving that is used when neither the form of the solution nor the path to it is clear in advance. Creativity requires neither judgment nor reason. It is purely inspirational, coming "out of the blue." In the 1960s many Western psychologists took the view that creativity involved the ability to identify relationships between ideas that were superficially very different from each other—the capacity to detect likeness in unlike things. To support this hypothesis, they devised the Remote Associates Test, in which the subject is provided with three words and asked to think of another word that is related to all three. For example, the word 'bite' is related to the three words widow, spider, and monkey. The tests certainly make an amusing parlor game, but do they reveal anything more than random verbal knowledge?

Thus far scientists have largely failed to identify the processes that lead to creative outcomes. Case studies of creativity depend too much on self-reports or after-the-event reconstructions to be reliable.

The work of Graham Wallas

One of the best-known and, for a while, most influential accounts of the human creative process appeared in *The Art of Thought* (1936), a posthumously published work by the English political scientist and psychologist Graham Wallas.

Wallas had the idea that part of problem solving may take place in our unconscious minds, rather than when we are actively thinking. He proposed that there are four separate stages of creative problem solving.
- *Preparation*. During the preparation stage the problem is investigated thoroughly. The mind attempts to solve the problem in many ways and becomes familiar with it.

Curriculum Context

Students should be able to explain the use of creative thinking in problem solving.

Portrait of a genius— the English playwright William Shakespeare (1564–1616). It is easier to describe his work than to know how it came into his mind and then found expression in his chosen medium.

Kekulé's Dream

Discoverers' explanations of how they came to make important breakthroughs seem to provide evidence for the importance of unconscious processes. One of the most famous examples is flash of inspiration that came to the German chemist August Kekulé in 1865. One evening he dreamed about snakes moving in circles and chasing their own tails. This gave him the idea that the chemical structure of benzene (C_6H_6) was a ring of six carbon atoms. Of course, it is difficult to be sure that it was really the dream that provided the key to the problem, because self-reporting is scientifically suspect.

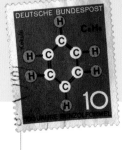

A German stamp from 1964 commemorates the discovery of the structure of benzene by August Kekulé. Kekulé said that he had the idea in a dream, but he told this story over 30 years after the discovery.

- *Incubation*. In the incubation period no conscious thought is given to the problem. However, the unconscious mind continues working on it.
- *Illumination*. This is the appearance of an apparently new solution to the problem. It may feel like a sudden insight.
- *Verification*. The problem-solver consciously tests to see if the new solution really does work.

At first sight these categories may appear entirely plausible, and sound like an accurate account of common experience. Yet much of the scientific basis of Wallas's work has since been discredited. Later researchers have denied the existence of an incubation stage: they prefer the "fresh start" explanation, which states that people find the right answer after they have had time to forget the wrong paths they originally took.

Improving creativity

Although it is not clear whether creativity can be increased, many people spend their time looking for ways to do so. In business one of the most commonly used techniques is brainstorming, or ideas meetings. Brainstorming involves first generating a large number of possible ideas and potential solutions to problems. All criticism and judgment are suspended during this period. Later, after many ideas have been generated, they are examined more carefully. The rationale behind brainstorming is that good ideas may be lost if a critical approach is adopted from the outset. Brainstorming is widely practiced in many industries, often successfully. Yet scientific studies of the effectiveness of the technique have produced mixed results. The main problem is that it increases the quantity of ideas, but it might fail to improve their quality.

Other techniques may also be involved in finding creative solutions. Thinking visually often seems to be important. A well-known example is that of Albert Einstein, who is reputed to have imagined himself traveling along a beam of light. That is said to have helped him develop his theory of relativity. The use of metaphors and analogies may also be useful. It is said that Alexander Graham Bell invented the telephone by thinking of possible mechanical equivalents to the organs in the human ear.

Reasoning, logic, rationality

Problem solving is only one part of thinking and reasoning. We turn now to an examination of people's ability to reason logically. There are many prescriptive theories about how people should reason—the rules they should follow in order to draw logical conclusions from various facts and premises. In practice, however, we do not always think in this way. This has led some psychologists to question whether we are really rational at all. Others see no paradox, believing that it is perfectly reasonable to be logical when necessary and intuitive at other times.

In everyday situations the use of perfectly accurate reasoning may not always be the best method of problem solving. Sometimes we have to make decisions quickly and may not have time to analyze a problem in detail. So perhaps rationality should be defined more broadly as the thought processes that

Curriculum Context

Students may be required to explain how cognitive processes, such as logical reasoning, are involved in intelligence.

Rationality
The quality of being based on reason or logic.

are most likely to help us achieve our goals. This is known as "satisficing." The idea behind satisficing, which was introduced by the economist and psychologist Herbert A. Simon, is that it is not always desirable to calculate a perfect solution, especially when it would take a long time to do so. The rational course is to stop looking for a better solution when the cost of continuing to search for it becomes greater than the potential benefits of finding it.

Boolean principles of thought

The Englishman George Boole (*see* box) is widely regarded as one of the founders of modern mathematics. In 1854 he published a book in which he attempted to define the principles of reasoning. One of his stated aims was "to investigate the fundamental laws of those operations of the mind by which reasoning is performed, [and] give expression to them in the symbolic language of a calculus." Boole assumed that the same rules of thinking could be applied in any area, not just in mathematics and logic.

Boole thought that the mind could be studied accurately only when it was working in a natural environment. He thought it important to ensure that studies of the human mind were always carried out in

George Boole

Born in 1815, George Boole was largely self-taught and never gained a university degree, but he still became one of the world's leading mathematicians. In an 1847 pamphlet Boole pointed out the analogy between algebraic symbols and symbols that can represent logical forms and syllogisms. He then made the revolutionary proposal that logic should be allied with mathematics rather than with philosophy.

Boole's work helped establish the foundations of symbolic logic, and today's digital computer circuits use a form of notation known as Boolean algebra. Many years after his death in 1865 Boole's ideas led to numerous applications he could never have imagined. Among them are telephone switching and electronic computers, which use the binary digits that Boole first developed.

normal, everyday circumstances. Much of his work can be seen as the forerunner of more recent, mainstream approaches to the study of the mind.

The work of Gigerenzer and others

During the second half of the 20th century detailed research into people's reasoning capacity increased scientific understanding of their problem-solving ability. Many psychologists, such as the German Gerd Gigerenzer, followed Boole and took the view that attempts to show that humans are irrational are flawed. Gigerenzer argued that people may perform some tasks badly because information is presented to them in an unnatural way or because they are interpreting the experimental task in a different way from the experimenter.

Another line of research has focused on various logical reasoning tasks. Again, much initial work appeared to show that people behave irrationally when facing such problems, but in the 1990s psychologist John Anderson and others suggested that we should talk about "adaptive rationality" rather than "normative rationality"—in other words, that we should describe somebody's behavior as rational if it is optimally adapted to the environment and context, even though it does not obey the rules of formal logic.

Probability

One important area of reasoning concerns people's judgment of probability. How likely is it that some future event will take place? If a horse has won its last five races, how does that affect its chances of winning a sixth? Probability theory, which can be used to answer such questions, was first developed between three and four hundred years ago. Gigerenzer and others have suggested that

Probability
Mathematical measurements of probability are expressed as numbers between 0 and 1, where 0 indicates that an event will never happen and 1 means it is certain to happen. For example, if you roll a die, the chances of it coming up on a particular number are 0.167 (1 in 6). If you draw a card randomly from a pack of 52, the probability of that card being the ace of clubs is about 0.02 (1 in 52).

Every time you throw a die, you have a 1 in 6 chance of your chosen number coming up.

An Eddy Test Example

Imagine a small town containing 1,000 women. One percent of the women (10) have cancer, while 99 percent (990) do not. All the women are tested for cancer. There is an 80 percent probability that a patient who has cancer will test positive. So 8 of the 10 who have cancer test positive, while 2 test negative. For the women who do not have cancer, there is a 10 percent chance of a false positive test. So 99 test positive, and 891 test negative. Overall, 107 women test positive: but only 8 of them really have cancer. Therefore, even a woman with a positive test has a less than 8 percent chance of actually having cancer.

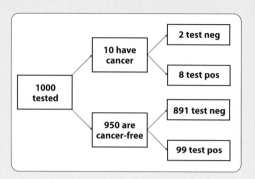

This diagram shows why, even if a woman has a positive breast cancer test, there is only an 8 percent chance that she actually has breast cancer.

our minds have not adapted well to dealing with information expressed as probabilities.

The Eddy Test

In a 1982 article the author and physician David M. Eddy found that even doctors are bad at estimating medical probabilities. Suppose you are a doctor, and you are examining a patient who has come to you after having noticed a lump in her breast. The woman has been sent for a mammogram and the test has come back positive. Your job is to tell your patient how likely it is that she has cancer, given the test result. You know the following three things:

- The probability that any woman being screened is suffering from breast cancer is 1 percent (0.01).
- If the patient has breast cancer, there is an 80 percent (0.8) probability that she will test positive (this is known as the "hit rate").
- If the patient does not have breast cancer, there is still a 10 percent (0.1) probability that she will test positive. This is known as the "false positive rate."

Mammogram

A test for breast cancer.

You now have to answer the question, "What is the probability that a patient with a positive test result actually has cancer?" With the figures above, most people would say that the chances are very high that a patient whose test is positive does have cancer. Most people estimate the chances at about 75 percent (0.75). In fact, the answer is only about 8 percent (0.08): in other words, the chances that the patient has cancer are extremely small, even with a positive test. This is because most patients (99 percent) do not have cancer, and so most of the positive tests are from women who do not have cancer but have a false positive test. Remember that 10 percent of cancer tests are false positives.

These findings are clearly of great practical significance. When doctors are asked questions of this nature, they typically make the error of assuming that a patient who tests positive is very likely to have the disease. In the breast cancer example the prior probability (base rate) is 1 percent—in other words, just one woman in a hundred has breast cancer before they are all tested. It is this evidence that is not taken into account in people's probabilistic reasoning. Similar examples can be found in many other areas.

HIV counseling

Research into HIV (human immunodeficiency virus) counseling provides another example of how a misunderstanding of probabilities can have serious medical consequences. In recent years it has become common to test low-risk populations for HIV. Gigerenzer and his colleagues examined a population in Germany in the 1990s. For the sample group, at that time, the probability of actually being HIV-positive even after having provided a positive test result was around 50 percent (0.5), i.e. about 1 in 2.

Gigerenzer investigated what actual advice was being given to people who tested positive for HIV. One of his

HIV (human immuno-deficiency virus)

A virus that causes the disease AIDS in humans. AIDS is an incurable disease that damages the immune system.

investigators went to 20 testing and counseling centers in Germany and received counseling on the interpretation of a possible positive test. One of the questions he asked was, "If one is not infected with HIV, is it possible to get a positive test result?" Most of the counselors answered incorrectly, saying that the chances were small or non-existent. A second question was "What is the probability that a man in my risk group actually has HIV after getting a positive test?" Fifteen out of twenty counselors replied "certain" or "almost certain," even though the actual probability was only about 50 percent.

Clearly this was a very serious finding. It illustrates an error of reasoning that could be damaging to the individual receiving incorrect advice.

Estimation of frequencies

Another well-established finding is that people systematically overestimate the chances of unlikely events happening and underestimate the chances that likely things will happen. For example, in 1978 researchers Paul Slovic, Baruch Fischhoff, and Sarah Lichtenstein asked people to estimate the frequency of various causes of death. People tended to think that the numbers killed in events such as tornadoes or floods were much greater than they in fact are. Conversely, people typically underestimated the number of deaths from common causes, such as heart disease and cancer.

Newspaper headlines after a severe earthquake in Haiti. People tend to overestimate the numbers of severe earthquakes because every one makes the news.

How do we account for such discrepancies between perception and reality? Several researchers have suggested that they occur because subjects rely on the availability of examples of the events in their memory. Deaths due to unusual causes are likely to be widely reported in the media, and as a result are more likely to be remembered. Deaths from more common causes are less newsworthy. Thus we are likely to recall more examples of deaths from unusual causes than of mundane, unreported causes of death.

Heuristics

A heuristic is a shortcut that people might use in problem solving or reasoning. Often, as we have seen, it is not possible to find the solution to a problem or to figure out the answers to a question in a completely systematic way. Even if such a solution were possible, it might take too long to compute. Kahneman and Tversky have therefore suggested that people may use heuristics to solve problems. The advantage of using a heuristic is that it will usually allow one to reach approximately the right answer to a problem quickly and without too much mental effort. The disadvantage is that in some circumstances a heuristic may lead to the wrong answer.

Curriculum Context

Students might be expected to provide examples of how heuristics is used in problem solving.

Decision making

Once people have—or believe they have—enough information about a problem, they make a decision. Such decisions are commonly informed by something known as the anchoring and adjustment heuristic. People who use it seem to estimate quantities or probabilities by starting with some initial number or estimate and then adjusting their estimate away from that starting point. However, they may not adjust enough. Some studies have found strong evidence of anchoring in the decisions made by consumers. For example, imagine running a promotion in which you offer cans of soup at a discount. You might put no limit on the number of cans of soup that can be purchased, or you may specify a maximum number per customer. One study, by psychologist Brian Wansink in the 1990s, found that the average number of cans of soup purchased during such a promotion was twice as high when the poster read "maximum 12 per customer" as it was when there was no stated limit.

Loss aversion

Several other reasoning biases can be illustrated by reference to consumer choices and purchasing. One is loss aversion. Essentially it means that losing money makes people more unhappy than gaining it. For example, consider how storekeepers might represent the fact that an item will cost more if the customer pays for it with a credit card. This situation can be presented as either a "cash discount" or a "credit card surcharge." Research has shown that people are more likely to use their credit card if the price difference is expressed as a cash discount, even though the price difference is the same in both cases. This is because "credit card surcharge" sounds like a loss and is therefore more unpleasant and worth avoiding.

A concept related to loss aversion is risk aversion. In general, people dislike risks but are more prepared to take them to prevent losses than to make gains.

Formal logic

In this final section we consider how people do and should perform on logical reasoning tasks. This has been investigated since the time of the ancient Greeks. Aristotle was concerned with a particular kind of reasoning known as deductive reasoning. For example, consider the following argument, the form of which is known as a syllogism:

All children are happy (first statement)
Andrew is a child (second statement)
Therefore Andrew is happy (conclusion)

A syllogism draws a conclusion from two statements. The rules of logic guarantee that you will end up with a true conclusion if the first two statements (the premises) are true. Therefore the correctness of the argument depends on two things: the truth of the premises and the structure of the argument being consistent with the rules of logic. In the example above, the argument structure is a good one. If it is true that all

Curriculum Context

Students should provide examples of how framing, risk avoidance, and overconfidence can affect decision making.

Curriculum Context

Students should examine the influence of the theories of Plato and other Greek philosophers on later Western studies of the mind.

children are happy, and it is also true that Andrew is a child, then the rules of logic provide an absolute guarantee that the conclusion (Andrew is happy) is also true. However, one of the premises of the argument (All children are happy) is false.

If we follow the rules of logic, we can guarantee that we will draw only accurate conclusions from true premises. These rules are very general; that is, they apply whatever the premises and conclusions are about. Consider the following rule:

$$P = Q$$

This is the logical notation meaning "if P is true, then Q is true." P and Q can each stand for any simple statement. For example, P could stand for "It is snowing," and Q might stand for "It is cold outside." The statement as a whole would then be: "If it is snowing, it is cold outside." But if we know that $P = Q$, this can help us draw other conclusions. For example, suppose we know that Q is not true. Then we can conclude that P is not true either. That is because the rule says that if P is true, then Q is true. If Q is not true, therefore, P must be untrue. This will remain the case whatever P and Q stand for. In the case of the specific example, we could conclude from "It is NOT cold outside" that "It is NOT snowing." The rules of logic are powerful because they can be applied to any statement.

Plato and Aristotle (right), as painted by the Renaissance artist Raphael. Aristotle's logic, especially his theory of the syllogism, has had an unparalleled influence on the history of Western thought.

Summary

In some of the studies in this chapter, people seem to reason incorrectly. Such findings have led some researchers to the conclusion that "humans are irrational." In many cases, however, people reason more correctly about probabilities when information is presented to them in what they regard as a natural way. As for creativity, while we may be able to describe some of its mechanics, its quintessence—for example, the inspiration that turns a painter from a journeyman into a genius—remains a mystery.

Glossary

Abstract Exisiting as an idea but having no physical existence.

Alzheimer's disease An incurable disease that causes loss of memory and other cognitive skills later in life.

Anterograde amnesia Inability to create memories after the episode that caused the amnesia.

Behaviorist perspective Behavioral psychologists argued that the mind could not be studied scientifically: Psychology should only concern itself with the way in which events in the world caused changes in animal (including human) behavior.

Bottom-up processing Information flowing from sensory input to the brain, to higher processing centers (the cerebral cortex).

Cerebral cortex The outer, folded layer of the brain, containing billions of nerve cells.

Cognitive Relating to the gaining of knowledge and understanding through thought, experience, and the senses.

Consciousness The mind's awareness of itself and the world.

Cornea The clear protective covering on the front of the eye.

CR The conditioned response, for example when a dog salivates in response to a bell that has become associated with food.

CS The conditioned stimulus. For example, the ringing of a bell just before a meal can become a CS if it comes to be associated with the imminent arrival of food.

Dichotic listening A procedure used in cognitive psychology that involves listening to two auditory streams, one in each ear.

Diencephalons A group of structures right in the center of the brain. For memory, the most important are the thalamus and the maxillary bodies.

Ethnic Relating to a group of people sharing a common culture or race.

Gender The state of being either male or female.

General Problem Solver (GPS) A computer program developed by Allen Newell, Herbert Simon, and J.C. Shaw that was designed to solve puzzles, and problems. However the program had no learning capability and its intelligence was only second-hand.

Gestalt psychologists The German word *Gestalt* means "form" or "whole." Gestalt psychologists saw the mind as a whole. They developed their ideas in the late 19th and early 20th centuries.

Heirarchy A system in which things or groups of things are ranked one above another according to status.

Hemisphere One of the two halves—left and right—of the brain.

Hertz (Hz) The frequency of sounds is measured in hertz (Hz), the number of vibrations per second. High frequency tones sound higher than low frequencies. Apart from octave gaps, frequencies that are close sound very similar, while widely separated frequencies sound completely different.

Hippocampus Part of the brain, thought to be the center of emotion and memory.

HIV (human immuno-deficiency virus) A virus that causes the disease AIDS in humans. AIDS is an incurable disease that damages the immune system.

Innate Present in all of us from birth.

Law of effect "Of several responses made to the same situation, those which are accompanied, or closely followed, by satisfaction to the animal will, other things being equal, be more firmly connected with the situation, so that, when it recurs, they will be more likely to recur; those which are accompanied or closely followed by discomfort to the animal will, other things being equal, have their connections with that situation weakened, so that, when it recurs, they will be less likely to recur." (Edward Thorndike)

Logic Reasoning conducted according to strict rules of validity.

Mammogram A test for breast cancer.

Mental representations The inner representations the mind holds of external objects or ideas.

Metaphor A figure of speech in which a word or phrase is used to mean something other than what it literally means.

Mind The thoughts, perceptions, memories, and emotions that make up human consciousness.

Neurons Brain cells specialized to conduct nerve impulses.

Neurotransmitters The chemicals that transfer impulses from one nerve fiber to another.

Objective Factual, unbiased information. The lengths and pitches of the notes in a piece of music are objective information. They do not depend on individual taste or opinion.

Operant conditioning Training a person or an animal to behave in a certain way by punishment or reward.

Physiology The study of the way living organisms and their body parts work.

Probability Mathematical measurements of probability are expressed as numbers between 0 and 1, where 0 indicates that an event will never happen and 1 means it is certain to happen. For example, if you roll a die, the chances of it coming up on a particular number are 0.167 (1 in 6). If you draw a card randomly from a pack of 52, the probability of that card being the ace of clubs is about 0.02 (1 in 52).

Rationality The quality of being based on reason or logic.

Reductionism Reductionism attempts to explain the processes of living organisms using physical laws usually applied to nonliving objects.

Retina The layer of light-sensitive cells on the inner surface of the eyeball.

Retrograde amnesia Inability to remember memories from before the episode that caused the amnesia.

Salivate Secrete saliva, a watery liquid that aids chewing, swallowing, and digestion.

Semantics The study of meaning in language.

Sibling A brother or sister.

Subjective A viewpoint that is based on personal experience and opinion. Taste in music, for example, is largely subjective.

Top-down processing When information from the senses is influenced by information stored in higher levels, for example experience.

UR The unconditioned response. For example, a dog might salivate in response to the sight or smell of food.

US The unconditioned stimulus. For example, food is a stimulus that makes a dog salivate in anticipation of a meal.

Visual cortex The part of the brain dealing with sight.

Further Research

BOOKS

Baddeley, A., Eysenck, M. W. and Anderson, M. C. *Memory*. London, UK: Psychology Press, 2010.

Bartlett, Frederick C. and Kintsch, Sir Walter *Remembering: A Study in Experimental and Social Psychology (2nd edition)*. Cambridge, UK: Cambridge University Press, 1995.

Boden, M. *Mind As Machine: A History of Cognitive Science* (2 volumes). New York: Oxford University Press, 2006.

Cardwell, M. *Dictionary of Psychology*. Chicago, IL: Fitzroy Dearborn Publishers, 2000.

Chomsky, N. and Arnove, A. *The Essential Chomsky*. New York: The New Press, 2008.

Davidson, J. E. and Sternberg, R. J. *The Psychology of Problem Solving*. Cambridge, UK: Cambridge University Press, 2003.

Eysenck, M. W. and Keane, M. T. *Cognitive Psychology: A Student's Handbook (6th Edition)*. London, UK: Psychology Press, 2010.

Fouts, R. and Tukel Mills, S. *Next of Kin: My Conversations with Chimpanzees*. London, UK: Harper Paperbacks, 1998.

Gazzaniga, M. S., Ivry, R. B., and Mangun, G. R. *Cognitive Neuroscience: The Biology of the Mind (2nd edition)*. New York: Norton, 2008.

Harley, T. A. *The Psychology of Language: From Data to Theory (2nd edition)*. Hove, UK: Psychology Press, 2008.

Hayes, N. *Psychology in Perspective (2nd edition)*. New York: Palgrave, 2002.

James, W. *Principles of Psychology*. New York: Cosimo Classics, 2007.

Kant, I. *Critique of Pure Reason*. London, UK: Penguin Classics, 2008.

Leahey, T. A. *A History of Psychology: Main Currents in Psychological Thought (6th edition)*. Upper Saddle River, NJ: Prentice Hall, 2003.

Lightbown, P. and Spasa, N. *How Languages Are Learned*. New York: Oxford University Press, USA, 2006.

Loftus, E. and Ketcham, K. *The Myth of Repressed Memory: False Memories and Allegations of Sexual Abuse*. New York: St. Martin's Griffin, 1996.

Pinker, S. *How the Mind Works*. New York: Norton, 2009.

Pinker, S. *Words and Rules: The Ingredients of Language*. New York: Basic Books, 1999.

Schwartz. T. *The Hillside Strangler: The Three Faces of America's Most Savage Rapist and Murderer and the Shocking Revelations from the Sensational Los Angeles Trial!* Fresno, CA: Linden Publishing, 2004.

Skinner, B.F. *About Behaviorism*. New York: Vintage, 1976.

Slater, L.: *Opening Skinner's Box: Great Psychological Experiments of the Twentieth Century*. London, UK: W. W. Norton & Company, 2005.

Styles, E. *The Psychology of Attention (2nd edition)*. London, UK: Psychology Press, 2006.

Todes, D. *Ivan Pavlov: Exploring the Animal Machine*. New York: Oxford University Press, USA, 2000.

Wittgenstein, L. *Philosophical Investigations (4th edition)*. Hoboken, NJ: Wiley-Blackwell, 2009.

Wundt, W. M. *An Introduction to Psychology—1912*. Ithaca, NY: Cornell University Library, 2009.

INTERNET RESOURCES

American Psychological Association. Here you can follow the development of new ethical guidelines for pscychologists, and find a wealth of other information.
www.apa.org

Association for Behavioral and Cognitive Therapies. An interdisciplinary organization concerned with the application of behavioral and cognitive sciences to the understanding of human behavior.
www.abct.org

Exploratorium. Click on "seeing" or "hearing" to check out visual and auditory illusions and other secrets of the mind.
www.exploratorium.edu/exhibits/nf_exhibits.html

Kidspsych. American Psychological Association's Children's site, with games and exercises for kids.
www.kidspsych.org/index1.html

Neuroscience for Kids. A useful website for students and teachers who want to learn about the nervous system. Enjoy activities and experiments on your way to learning all about the brain and nervous spinal cord.
faculty.washington.edu/chudler/neurok.html

Neuroscience Tutorial. The Washington University School of Medicine's online tutorial offers an illustrated guide to the basics of clinical neuroscience, with useful artworks and user-friendly text.
thalamus.wustl.edu/course

Social Psychology Network. One of the largest social psychology databases on the Internet. Within these pages you will find more than 5,000 links to psychology-related resources and research groups, and there is also a useful section on general psychology.
www.socialpsychology.org

Index

Page numbers in *italic* refer to illustrations and captions.

A

a priori concepts 11
Abelson, Robert 55
acoustic signal 82–83
ADD (attentional deficit disorder) 29–30
aging and memory 75–76
Allport, D. A. 25
Alzheimer patients 76
amnesia 76–77
analogies 94, 97
anchoring and adjustment 103
Anderson, John 99
Anderson, Paul 23
anterior cingulated cortex 31
anterograde amnesia 76
Antonis, B. 25
aphasia 81
Aristotle 46, *105*
associative learning 33, 35, 53, 54
attention 9, 13, *14*, 15, 16, 18–31, 39, 41, 59, 60, 69, 70, 73, 76
attention bottleneck 18, *18*, 20, 21, 22
attentional disorders 28–29
attenuation theory (of attention) 21–22
Ayllon, Teodoro 43, 44
Azrin, Nathan 43, 44

Β

babbling 86
Bartlett, Sir Frederick 57, 66, 67, 68
Bartlett tradition 67
behavior therapy 43, 44
behaviorism 7, 15, 43
Bell, Alexander Graham 97
Bianchi, Kenneth 77
bird, definitions 50, 51–53
Black, John 55
Boole, George 98, 99
Boolean principles 98–99
bottom-up processing 9, 83
Bower, Gordon 55, 56
brain capacity 18

brain damage 17, 76, 77, 81
brain imaging 81, 82
brainstorming 96–97
breast cancer 100–101
Broadbent, Donald 20, 21, 22
Broca, Paul 81

C

categories 50–51, 53, 54, 64, 74, 76, 91, 96
cats and problem solving 37–38, 90, 91
central nervous system 62
cerebral cortex 30, 62, 77, 81
Cherry, Colin 19, 20
chess positions, memorizing 68
chess problems 93
child abuse 72
chimpanzees 78–79, 80
Chomsky, Noam 80
classical conditioning 32–33, 34, 35, 36, 37
click languages 80
cocktail party effect 13–14, 20–21, 60
cognitive neuroscience 27, 28, 31
cognitive psychologists 7, 8, 10, 11, 14, 16
cognitive psychology 6, 10, 13, 16
Collins, Allan 52
computer programs 6, 7, 8, 9, 13, 16, 57, 59, 60, 94
computer view of the mind 9, 16, 60, 94
conditioned response (CR) 34, 35
conditioned stimulus (CS) 34, 35
conditioning 32–45
connectionist theory 57
context retrieval 64, 75
Corbetta, Maurizio 28
cornea 6
Craik, Fergus 61
creativity 79, 90, 95, 96, [105]
creoles *88*
cued recall 64, 65, 68

D

deaths, causes of 102–103
decision making 15, 90, 92, 103, 104
defining attributes 49, 50, 51
Dehaene, Stanislas 28
dementia 76
Descartes, René 11
Deutsch, J. and D. 22
development of memory 74–75
dichotic listening 19, 20, 21
dictionaries in the brain 49–51, 52
diencephalon 76, 77
discourse 83, 84
discourse processing 83
distraction 25, 30, 31
divided attention 24–25
dogs, Pavlov's 32, 33, 34, 35
doodles 54, *54*
driving 25, 26
duck–rabbit drawing *48*

E

Ebbinghaus, Hermann 66, 72
Ebbinghaus tradition 66–67
Eddy, David M. 100
Eddy test 100, *100*
EEG (electroencephalogram) 17, 27
Einstein, Albert 97
electric shock conditioning 35
encoding (memory) 58, 59, 60, 63, 64, 69, 74, 75
episodic memory 63
errors in memory 69
experience, effect of 15, 25, 26, 33, 66
experts, expertise 27, 68, 73, 94
explicit memory 63, 64, 65, 76
external representations 46, 48
extinction 34, 40
eyewitness testimony 69–70

F

familiarity retrieval 64, 75
feature integration theory (FIT) 23, 24

feature-associative network 53–54, *53*
filter theory (of attention) 20
Fischhoff, Baruch 102
fMRI (functional magnetic resonance imaging) 17, 27, *31*, 47
forgetting 65, 66, 65, 67
formal logic 104–105
Frege, Gottlob 49, 51
frequency estimation 102
fugue state 77
Fuller, Linda 43
functional fixity 91–92

G

Galton, Francis, 46
Gemsbacher, Morton *48*
General Problem Solver (GPS) 15, 94
generalization 34, 87
Genie 89
Gestalt psychology 7, 15, 90
Gigerenzer, Gerd 99, 101
Glucksberg Sam 50
grammar 16, 80, 82, 88

H

Hayes-Roth, Barbara 49
hearing in the womb *86*
Herbert A. Simon 15, 93, 94, 98
heuristics 103
hierarchies 9, 52, *52*, 81
hippocampus 62, *62*, 76, 77
HIV counselling 101–102
Homa, Donald 54
honeybees 78
Hume, David *10*, 11
Humphreys, Duncan and Glyn 24

I

illumination 96
illusory conjunction 23
implicit memory 63, 74, 75
improving memory 72–73
incubation 96
influencing memory 71–72
information processing 6, 7, 8, 9, 12, 14, 16, 18–31, 61
insight 15, 38, 90–91, 96

instrumental conditioning 37
intentionality 15
internal representations 46, 48
introspection 10
Isabelle 89
isolated children 89

J

Jones, Mary Cover 36

K

Kant, Emmanuel 11, 12
Kekulé, August 96, *96*
key-pecking in pigeons 45
Kintsch, Walter 83
Köhler, Wolfgang 90
Kosslyn, Stephen 47

L

language 9, 15, 16, 20, 45, 62, 74, 76, 78–89
language acquisition 85–87
language processing 16, 78–89
law of effect 38
laws of learning 34
leading questions 70, *70*
learning 32, 33, 34, 35, 37, 38, 44, 45, 54, 63, 65, 66, 67, 68, 72, 90, 94
levels of processing framework 60–61
Lichtenstein, Sarah 102
Locke, John 11
Lockhart, Robert 61
Loftus, Elizabeth 71
logical reasoning 97, 99
long-term memory 14, 15, 59, 60, 61, 62, 63, 66, 75, 76, 77, 83, 84
loss aversion 104
Luria, A. R. 59

M

McClosky, Michael 50
Maier, N. R. F. 91, 92
mammograms 100–101
means-end analysis 93
memory 9, 10, 14–15, 17, 58–77, *71*, *75*, 83, 84, 102

mental dictionaries 53
mental images 46–48
mental maps 48–49
mental representations 15
method of loci 73
mind 6, 10, 14, 15, 16
mistaken identity 69
mnemonics 73–74
modal model of memory *61*
morpheme 80, 81
motivation to learn 72
multiple personality disorder 77

N

neglect syndrome 28–29
neurons 7, 17, 57
neurotransmitters 30
Newell, Allen 15, 93, 94
nonhuman language 78–79
nonsense syllables 59, 66, 67, 72

O

objections to behaviour therapy 44–45
operant conditioning 32, 38–39, 41, 42, 43, 44, 45
operant conditioning chamber ("Skinner Box") 38

P

pain 30–31, 35
parsing 84
Pavlov, Ivan 32, 33, *33*, 34, 35, 45
peg words 73, 74
perfect memory 59
PET (positron emission tomography) 17, 27, 28, 30, 31
pheromones 78
phobias 36–37
phoneme 80, *81*, 82, 83, *83*, 86
pidgins *88*
pigeon behavior 39, *39*
Plato 58, *105*
positive punishment 41, 44
positive reinforcement 39
Posner, Michael 28, 29

probability 39, 90, 99–100, 101, 102
problem solving 9, 15, 16, 17, 38, 90–105
problems of arrangement 91
problems of transformation 92–93
psychoanalysis 7
psycholinguists 78
psychological damage 77
puzzle boxes 37–38

Q

Quillian, Ross 52

R

rRAM (random-access memory) 60
Ramu 89
rationality 97, 99
rats, experiments on 35, 38, 39
reaction times 12–13
reading 84–85
recall 55, 59, 60, 63, 64, 65, 67, 68, 69, 70, 75, 103
recognition 63, 64, 65, 75
reconstructive nature of memory 67, 68
Remote Associates Test 95
representing information 46–57
restaurant scripts 55
retina 6
retrieval (memory) 59, 60, 61, 63, 64, 65, 68
retrograde amnesia 76
rewards 41
Reynolds, P. 25
Rips, Lance 53
Ritalin 30, 31
river-crossing problems 92
Romeo and Juliet 56, *56*
Rosch, Eleanor 50, 51, *51*
Rubin vase *9*
Russell, Bertrand 50

S

salivary responses 32, 33, 34, 35
satisficing 98
Schank, Roger 55, 56
scripts and themes 54–56

secondary reinforcers 40–41
Seifert, Colleen 56
selective attention 19, 20, *20*, 21, 24, 28
semantic memory 63, 75
sensory memory (transitional memory, sensory store) 14, 20, 22, 60, 61
Shakespeare, William 56, *95*
shaping *42*, 43
Shaw, J. C. 94
Shereshevskii 59
Sherlock Holmes 11, *12*
Shoben, Edward 53
short-term memory *see* working memory
sign language 78
similarity theory 24
Simon, Herbert 15, 93, 94
Simonides 73
Skinner, B. F. 38, 39, *39*, 43, 44, 45
Slovic, Paul 102
Smith, Edward 53
speech 16
state-space 92
Stenman, Evald 23
Sterling, Sharon 54
stimulus control 42–43
storage (memory) 59, 60, 74
storage limitations 65
stories, remembering 56–57, 68
Stroop effect 26, 27
structure of language 79–80
subtasks 26, 27
suprasegmentals 80
syllables 80
syllogisms 104–105
synesthesia 59
syntax 79

T

Thompson, Donald 69
Thorndike, Edward Lee 37, 90, 91
Thorndyke, Perry 49
"tip of the tongue phenomenon" 63
token economy 43–44
top-down processing *9*, 83
transcendental method 11, 12
transitional memory *see* sensory memory

Treisman, Anne 21, 22, *22*, 23
Trepe, Lawrence 54
trial and error 15, 37, 38, 90–91
Turner, Terrance 55
two-word sentences 87
typical and atypical members 51

U

unconditioned response (UR) 33, 35
unconditioned stimulus (US) 33, 34, 35
understanding language 82–83
unlikely events 102–103

V

verification 96
vision 6, 7, 13
visual cortex 6, 7, 9, 17, 47
visual search 22–23, 28
vocabulary 87
von Wright, Elsa 23

W

Wallas, Graham 95–96
War of the Ghosts 67
Wasnink, Brian 103
Wernicke, Carl 81
West Side Story 56, *56*
wild children 89
Wittgenstein, Ludwig 49, 50
Wolpe, Joseph 36
working memory 14, 20, 22, 60, 61, 75, 83
Wundt, Wilhelm 10